MANY
OICES
MANY
PPORTUNITIES
CULTURAL PLURALISM
& AMERICAN ARTS POLICY

CLEMENT ALEXANDER PRICE

MANY VOICES
MANY OPPORTUNITIES

CULTURAL PLURALISM & AMERICAN ARTS POLICY

FOREWORD BY DR. BILLY TAYLOR

acabooks

AMERICAN COUNCIL FOR THE ARTS
New York, New York

Copublished with Allworth Press

This project was made possible
through the generous support
of the Ford Foundation.

Copyright © 1994 American Council for the Arts

Published by the American Council for the Arts
One East 53rd Street, New York, N.Y. 10022.

Director of Publishing: Robert Porter
Assistant Director of Publishing: Julia Dubner
Edited by Barbara Ryan, Editorial Associates
Book and cover design by Celine Brandes, Photo Plus Art

Library of Congress Cataloging-in-Publication data
Price, Clement Alexander, 1945-
   Many voices, many opportunities: cultural pluralism
and American arts policy / Clement Alexander Price.
        p. cm.
   Includes bibliographical references.
   ISBN 1-879903-16-4
   1. United States—Cultural policy. 2. Ethnic
arts—United States. 3. Multiculturalism—United States.
4. Arts and society—United States—History—20th
century. I. Title.
NX705.5.U6P75   1993
700'.1'03—dc20   93-34290
                                            CIP

In Memory of Don Miller
Friend, Mentor and Artist of the African Diaspora

Contents

LIST OF PHOTOGRAPHY CREDITS

CHAPTER 1

All photographs in this chapter, except for the one on page 15, are from the Archives Center, National Museum of American History, Smithsonian Institution.

Page 4: Mechanics Band, Smithsonian Institution Photo Number 87-14213, photographer unidentified; Universal Black Band, Smithsonian Institution Photo Number 87-14212, photographer unidentified; both from the Hazen Collection of Band Photographs and Ephemera.
Page 9: Smithsonian Institution Photo Number 87-14133, albumen cabinet print by Gurley & Harris, from the Hazen Collection of Band Photographs and Ephemera.
Page 15: Photographer unidentified, courtesy of the Newark Public Library.
Page 17: Photographer unidentified, from the United Shoe Machinery Company Records.

CHAPTER 2

All photographs in this chapter, except for the one on page 22, are from the Archives Center, National Museum of American History, Smithsonian Institution.

Page 22: Photographer unidentified, courtesy of the Newark Public Library.
Page 24: Smithsonian Institution Photo Number 83-16713, photographer unidentified, from the George H. Clark Radioana Collection.

Foreword

Whenever I hear people speak of multiculturalism, I think of my own schooling. I went to Dunbar High School in Washington, D.C., an all-black school, where we had five people with doctorate degrees on the faculty. These people were on our high school faculty because they couldn't teach at Harvard and Yale and other places where they should have been teaching. But the one thing that they imparted to their students was that as a group they had something of which to be proud. I thought Marian Anderson and Roland Hayes and Paul Robeson came to everybody's school. They came to mine.

They gave us concrete examples of people who looked like us, who had achieved great things, who we could use as models.

They also showed us that those same people were people of courage and people of great intellect.

I recall that one of my teachers, Mary Reese Europe, took several of us athletic fellows who were trying to be basketball and football players and told us, in a music class, that if we were really talking about personal courage we should think of Roland Hayes. Roland Hayes went to Germany in 1921 to do a concert and was hooted and booed. The Germans felt, "How dare this man of African descent come and try to sing our music." But he stood in this large concert hall and waited them out. It was obvious he wasn't going anywhere, and if they didn't want him to be there, they would have to leave. They didn't leave, and when they finally became quiet, he sang for them. Once he sang for them, the beauty of his voice, his wonderful artistry, captured them; it reached their hearts. By singing, he said something to them that he couldn't say in their own language just by talking. He proved that he could communicate as an artist in a multicultured way. That was a very important lesson for me, and for many years I often wondered what kind of person it took—and the type of training to nurture the talent—that enabled him to do that.

The arts have always been a basic and effective medium of human communication and understanding. When we speak of cultural pluralism in American life, we can begin with American jazz as an excellent example. Jazz is America's classical music. It is a musical language, and it has developed from a single expression of the consciousness of black people to a national music which expresses Americana to Americans as well as American ideals to people from other cultures.

As a classical music with its own standards of form, complexity, literacy and excellence, jazz has been a major influence on the music of the world for more than 100 years. Because jazz has utilized and restructured materials from many other musical traditions, there's a style of jazz that sounds like European classical music, a style of jazz that sounds like country and western music, a style of jazz that sounds like East Indian classical music, and styles of jazz that reflect the cultural input of many various other kinds of music found in this country and elsewhere in the world.

Jazz emerged from the need of African-Americans to express themselves in musical terms. This need for self-expression stems directly from the African musical heritage. In African societies, music was essential in cementing together a culture, perpetuating cultural continuance, enforcing the moral and spiritual order, allowing an individual to express oneself and helping an individual adjust to group norms. As a result, though Africans were stripped of almost everything else when they were brought to America as slaves, they brought with them a shared tradition of using music to accompany and define all the activities of life—there was music for working, for playing, for hunting, for religious activities, social activities and much more. Africans retained and restructured their cultural traditions as survival tools, and jazz was derived from traditions and aesthetics that were non-European in origin and concept.

Jazz defines our national culture, and it serves in a sense as a musical mirror, reflecting who and what Americans were, in their own view, at different points in their development. It's something that's very special, and it does have an influence on people all over the world.

The one aspect of jazz that I think reflects the American tradition best is improvisation, doing your own thing within the structure of that particular music. Some years ago I was in Europe giving a concert, and a man came backstage and he said, "I really am interested in what you do, what you have to say, the political point of view you make." Well, I don't think of my music as being particularly political, so I didn't know what he was talking about. What he was talking about was the fact that, as the leader of a jazz trio, I walk out on stage and say, "We're going to play such and such a tune;" I go sit down at the piano, and once I begin to play, the other two members, the bassist and the drummer, obviously have as much to do with the final product as I do. It's a very democratic process.

Classical music must be time-tested, it must serve as a standard or model, it must have established value and it must be indigenous to the culture for which it speaks. Jazz meets that criteria, yet many Americans have been consistent in their bias against it. They believe that Western classical music is superior to any other kind of music in the world, and therefore that it is the only music that warrants serious and intensive study. This belief has resulted in the systematic exclusion of jazz and other African-American music from much of the American cultural experience.

As a pianist-composer I've played and had my music played all over the world, so I can speak from that experience about the impact of jazz on other cultures. America is culturally rich, but we are a wasteful nation. We are wasting talent, facilities, money and opportunities. We need to identify artists and potential artists from all ethnic groups and help them learn as much as possible about their own traditions and their own cultures. We need to help them find appropriate and effective ways to develop and share their creativity with the rest of us. We need to provide the broadest range of cultural experience to our children. They must be encouraged to participate in the arts throughout their school years. And we must find the motivation and money to institute this policy immediately. It's already too late for many of our young people.

Most Americans get their cultural experiences from radio and television. Instead of deploring what's available, we collectively and individually need to work more effectively to make the communications media more responsive to our cultural needs. This is the only country in the world where the public supposedly owns the airwaves, yet we don't insist that they do more.

Clement Price has given us much to think about in the pages that follow, and I sincerely hope that it will stimulate a concentrated effort toward devising more effective ways to bypass semantics, and ethnic and cultural bias, and to help the entire cultural community of artists and organizations move forward toward a more effective national arts policy.

Dr. Billy Taylor

Preface

rtists and those who represent their interests are hardly strangers to the controversies that inevitably arise when the antecedents and character of contemporary American culture are discussed. From the earliest years of America's history as a multi-racial society, creative people were products of Old World backgrounds and agents for diversity; they were also pivotal figures articulating the unique qualities of an evolving culture. Artists have been among the American society's most avid boosters for innovation inspired by different voices. When the arts became institutionalized at the turn of this century, artists often worked in arenas where creative people learned from one another across the barriers of race, social class, gender and national origin. Indeed, the tendency of the arts to accept and benefit from the cross fertilization of cultures has been one of the reasons why so many historically marginalized people have considered arts organizations as havens.

But despite the openness of American creativity to cultural differences, the arts have been increasingly drawn into the contemporary debate over the relationship between social, political and economic inequities and cultural hegemony. As public support for the arts increased after the establishment of the National Endowment for the Arts, that debate became more intense and acrimonious.

This study examines the broad historical and intellectual changes that set the stage for the current dialogue over arts policy in the United States and the relationship that exists between selected aspects of historical change and the rise of cultural pluralism as a modus operandi in the arts. It is, in short, a historical musing on how the past influences the way Americans now think about their diverse cultures and resulting influences on how the arts are supported.

What follows started out as a very short paper on the responsibility of arts organizations to the diverse communities they serve, delivered in 1990 at a conference in Newark, New Jersey sponsored by the American Council for the Arts. At the time my arguments were informed by more than ten years as a volunteer to various arts organizations. In retrospect, those views are still valid, but in the pages that follow I look more critically at the reasons why diversity must be taken seriously as a permanent feature of arts policy development and presentation. Equally important, I try to provide some historical insights that might be useful for arts professionals who find themselves caught up in the passions that mark the so-called culture wars.

My involvement in promoting the support and appreciation of the arts in the United States coincided with a professional interest in making the study of American history useful to professionals in not-for-profit arts and humanities organizations in my local community. It began during the late 1970s, when I was appointed to the New Jersey State Council on the Arts. In New Jersey, and in other states at the time, the swift winds of demographic change were forcing arts institutions to broaden their audiences, expand their repertoire, and desegregate their fiduciary boards. Cultural democracy, which had long been an objective of minority artists and intellectuals, seemed to mimic the much older ideal of political democracy. As a student of Afro-American and urban history, it seemed to me that many of the dilemmas facing arts professionals could be better addressed through an enhanced understanding of America's racial and ethnic minorities and a recognition that revisionist historiography was of value to an understanding of changes in the society.

Since I am to a great extent an outsider to professional arts management, I am indebted to many old friends and colleagues in the American public arts movement who have shared with me their aspirations and problems. I would especially like to express my deepest appreciation to Milton Rhodes, the president of the American Council for the Arts, whose encouragement and support helped me expand upon the presentation I delivered in 1990. Milton is among a few outstanding American arts leaders who believes that arts development in the nation can benefit from perspectives found in other disciplines and from outsiders such as myself. I also want to thank Linwood J. Oglesby, the executive director of ACA, who, along with Milton, carefully read and gave valuable criticisms to the earlier drafts. Over the months that I sought to hone my arguments for readers unaccustomed to looking at arts policy from the vantage point of history, I relied on the thoughtful suggestions of Leon Denmark, Victor Davson, Anna M. Aschkenes, Giles R. Wright, Sondra H. Myers, Lonnie Bunch, Mark M. Murphy, and Jeffrey A. Kesper. My selection of photographs was assisted greatly by Camille Thomas of the National Endowment for the Arts, David Haberstich and John A. Fleckner of the Smithsonian Institution, and Charles Cummings of the Newark Public Library. Robert Porter, director of policy, planning and publishing for ACA, was instrumental in guiding the manuscript to publication, and over many months he was the person most successful in keeping me focused on the project amidst many other competing responsibilities. I could not have had a better, nor a more patient, editor. And, finally, let me thank my wife, Mary Sue Sweeney, who generously gave me the kind of encouragement and counsel I needed to explore ideas about arts policy that I had not previously considered.

There is always a risk of missing the point when a writer takes on a project better tackled by a specialist. As an arts volunteer who has watched arts professionals cope with the pressures imposed by declining financial support, competition from popular forms of entertainment and antagonisms across racial and cultural lines, I must admit to a sense of inadequacy. Yet, at the same time, there is perhaps much to be gained by looking at an old issue, such as the diversity question, through the work of a friendly outsider. In that spirit this book was written.

Clement Alexander Price
Newark, New Jersey
January 1994

1

Collective Memory and the Culture Line in American Life

For the longest time many Americans have been deeply troubled and combative over the nature and authenticity of our nation's past and culture. There has been a struggle over the history and memory of the American people. Traditionally, our history was shaped by a narrative and consensus approach to the past, a litany of outstanding democratic achievements made over time largely by the English stock of American immigrants. This line of historical reasoning was clearly not without value in a developing society, for it rationalized, during periods of great conflict, the uniqueness of the American experiment with freedom and justice. America was viewed not only as a success story for most of its citizens but also as a land blessed with extraordinary natural and human resources, a new kind of society. What made this view especially alluring to succeeding generations of Americans was its neatness, its lack of conflicting images, its circumvention of great failures and tragedies.

Yet over the course of the twentieth century, the traditional vistas of our past were challenged as the history of the American people was broadened to include an array of experiences that had been largely invisible because of their disturbing meaning. This approach, to look at the past from as many vantage points as possible, has become the basis for a new American history. America, according to this line of historical reasoning, has been characterized largely by conflict between those who acquired democratic rights and those who were denied such rights. Considerations of the importance of race, class, gender and culture have figured prominently in this view of America as a society marked by conflict. Equally important, such considerations have become the basis for difficult discussions on what the past has made of our democracy.

For the earliest English-speaking settlers and for successive generations of their descendants, the past was a utilitarian rationalization of the present and future. They needed to view the broad sweep of American history through the rather narrow prism of their experiences, their culture. During the early years of U.S. history, British-American colonists, fearing that their errand in the wilderness was fraught with the real and imagined dangers of life among Indians and Africans, and becoming all the more convinced that their vision of America as a white man's land was imperiled, sought desperately to keep alive their Old World customs. The lands of Native Americans were largely appropriated and the customs of the aboriginal population were weakened over time. At the same time, the Africans,

far away from their native lands and cultures, were kept beyond the pale of American society through generations of bond-
age and racial exclusion. Against this colonial background, the
young nation's hunger for white racial destiny led to an expan-
sionist war with Mexico. Later the labor of the Chinese was ex-
ploited in the Western territories and, when their numbers
threatened the power of the white population, they were kept
out by legislative fiat. These often brutal acts of racial and cultural expansion were sanctioned by historical and cultural visions that generally reflected those of the white majority,
especially the Anglo-American need for recognizable standards
of civilization, growth and supremacy.

This underside of American history existed in the face of
a pervasive belief in our nation's diversity, a belief given eloquent expression by early American writers, including Michel
Guillaume Jean de Crèvecoeur, Ralph Waldo Emerson and Her-
man Melville, among others. They envisioned a new kind of society, a nation forged out of the world's diverse cultures, a
"federated whole," as Emerson put it. The nation's democratic
ideals, brought to the surface during the ages of Jefferson,
Jackson and Lincoln, encouraged many Anglo-Americans,
amid the establishment of a racial hierarchy that debased Native Americans and immigrants of color, to espouse intercultural tolerance.

Beneath the veneer of that powerful ideal there always existed a prevailing view of America's past which nurtured a delu-
sion about our society, its people and its cultures. The view
held that this society, despite its rich array of colors, cultures
and historical experiences, was best understood from the vantage point of what the English-speaking settlers and their

**Mechanics Band, Antrim, New York, ca. 1890 and
Universal Black Band, Newark, New Jersey, ca. 1900.**

progeny accomplished, wrote about and planned to do. That dominant view encouraged great patriotic oratory because it indulged the remarkable achievements of those who most influenced the nation's memory and its economic, educational and political institutions. It fueled our optimism as an ostensibly united people.

Although the United States was not as brutal to the indigenous population and the forced immigrants as other European settler nations in the New World, its perceptions of the past produced enormous anxieties within the dominant population. Having been driven by the notion that their society was blessedly unique in its abundant opportunities for all and in its reverence for individual freedom, Anglo-Americans could never bring themselves to look into the chasm, into the void of their past—that major part of their history in which some cultures were nearly crushed. Nor could many Americans ever bring themselves to an understanding of what the aboriginals and darker ethnics actually thought about the integrity of their own cultures. Seemingly always uncomfortable with the darker groups in their midst, many U.S.-born whites believed that it was their culture, not that of the others, which was threatened in a multiracial, multiethnic society. With such beliefs, the ideals of freedom, justice, equality, opportunity and optimism were calibrated along the color line. Freedom for black men, it was feared, imperiled freedom for white men, which probably contributed to the belief widely held by white Americans that any attempt to elevate the social and political status of blacks, reds and browns was potentially dangerous. During the colonial period and through much of the nineteenth century, most white Americans envisioned that the emancipation of Africans would result in a debauched and motley society. That is to say, black freedom would cause a sharp increase in racial intermixing and hence virtually capsize Caucasian civilization. "What is arresting about this opinion," Winthrop Jordan writes, "is that no one attempted to give reasons why such a development was inevitable and that there were in fact no good reasons."

There were also no acceptable reasons for the generalized view that aboriginal Americans were wild beasts, unreasonable creatures and brutish savages, a view that was tempered only after Native American societies had been considerably weakened by generations of disease, warfare, social pathology and dislocation.

In deluding themselves so profoundly about the often frightening cultures they lived among in the American wilderness, on the frontier and on the streets of the burgeoning cities of the nineteenth century, Americans could go but so far in redressing the grievances of the past. By the early nineteenth century, Anglo-Americans admitted their own prejudice, but in so doing they claimed that racial prejudice against colored people was so pervasive only time would eradicate it. The darker skinned groups probably recognized that the rationalization of their debasement portended a rough road ahead, as indeed it did. They were increasingly forced into unreasonable accommodations to the inevitable prejudice of the majority population. The Native Americans, facing the terrible

Freedom for black men, it was feared, imperiled freedom for white men, which probably contributed to the belief widely held by white Americans that any attempt to elevate the social and political status of blacks, reds and browns was potentially dangerous.

prospect of near extermination, virtually admitted defeat in the control of their destiny by retreating to the reservations. The Africans, having all but given up on the prospect of a return to their native lands, which was as strong a sentiment among that group as staying in the United States, chose the unenviable course of attempting to advance themselves in the face of overwhelming white resistance to both black self-determination and assimilation. The Chinese would remain largely invisible until the mid-twentieth century; the Mexicans would exist between two societies, one terribly poor, the other virtually closed to them. Two generations later Japanese Americans, viewed as a potential threat to domestic security during World War II, were denied their civil rights and interned in relocation camps. And the white ethnics, those who benefitted from the external quality of light pigmentation in a society contemptuous of dark skin, would in varying degrees jettison part of their former selves and become, as James Baldwin was to observe much later, simply whites.

The legacy of racial and cultural intolerance, sustained over time as much by the tenacity of group prejudice as by the extraordinary achievements of European immigrants to America, came under close scrutiny and growing criticism during the modern age, at a time when racism was coming under increasingly effective attack and when darker ethnic groups, especially the descendants of African slaves, produced their first generation of scholars and artists. Progressive reforms during the early twentieth century were beneficial to the nation's darker citizens and gave them a voice in public affairs that had been denied to their forebears. Indeed, the dark ethnic groups, in asserting that the old intolerances blunted their promise in American life, were beginning a grand assault on the colonial and nationalistic notion of America as a white man's land and its culture as solely a product of Anglo influences.

Moreover, as one measure of what a society is capable of understanding about itself, historical and behavioral scientific scholarship increasingly questioned the idea of racial and cultural supremacy. In 1903, in one great and lasting stroke of insight, the young Negro historian W.E.B. DuBois observed that "the problem of the twentieth century is the problem of the color line—the relation of the darker to the lighter races of men in Asia and Africa, in America and the islands of the sea."

> **In 1903, in one great and lasting stroke of insight, the young Negro historian W.E.B. DuBois observed that "the problem of the twentieth century is the problem of the color line—the relation of the darker to the lighter races of men in Asia and Africa, in America and the islands of the sea."**

As this dramatically eventful and often disturbing century draws to a close, DuBois, with those now famous words, was prophetic when we consider what "color" has come to mean in the United States. Indeed, three generations of persistent resistance to racial injustice, coupled with the expansion and study of the behavioral sciences, the arts and humanities, have fostered intense ethnic consciousness among many Americans. In this sense, even those of Protestant stock have become "ethnic" because there exists a critical scrutiny of their racial and cultural distinctiveness that would have been unthinkable a century ago. At the same time, ethnic consciousness among other groups, especially the progeny of European immigrants who entered the United States during the nineteenth and early twentieth centuries, has waned or, perhaps, been transformed into transethnic white solidarity and postmodern racism. The dramatic increase in the number of foreign-born Americans in the population in recent years has not only made possible such sentiments but also encouraged a healthy discussion of the process by which newcomers become Americans in their cultural and social aspirations.

Female cornetist with B-flat instrument, Utica, New York, ca. 1880.

By the early twentieth century, two interpretations sought to explain the process of intercultural contact: the idea of the Melting Pot and cultural pluralism. The Melting Pot is now generally recognized as a glorious myth, in which America is seen as the "land of freedom, democracy, and golden opportunity in which people of all races, creeds, and colors are accepted on equal terms." It assumes that the assimilation or fusion of huge numbers of immigrants is a vital objective of American history and culture.

> **By the early twentieth century, two interpretations sought to explain the process of intercultural contact: the idea of the Melting Pot and cultural pluralism.**

Cultural pluralism, which, at least at the moment, has the greatest support among ethnic advocates in American society, has traditionally espoused the belief that all cultures are relatively equal and should participate equally in a diverse society, that our culture is derivative of many influences and "that our diversity brings us a special strength and vitality." It seeks an end to both cultural animosities and Anglo-centered assimilation.

♦ ♦ ♦ ♦

The willingness of growing numbers of Americans to confront old cultural and historical prejudices with new ideas and with more compassion than was possible before the two World Wars helped guide the great changes between the 1950s and the 1970s. The modern civil rights movement, easily the nation's most significant twentieth-century social reform, was both the catalyst for a broader vision of American democracy and the most obvious beneficiary of the new thinking about culture, the beneficent role of activist government, the relative worth of ethnic groups, and America's image in the darker parts of the world.

The civil rights movement gave cultural pluralism a revitalized voice and a social, political and cultural agenda. The idea became more passionate, more distinctly ideological and, to some, more threatening. On the many battlefields on which the civil rights movement was fought—the right of equal opportunity in voting, housing, employment and education—cultural pluralism was powerfully transformed into a potent movement for change.

Many sectors of American society, including the arts, now face the inevitable tensions that arise when the ideals of cultural pluralism take on a political character. This is so because we live in a post-civil rights era, a time when political rights, having been won by all Americans, are viewed by recent beneficiaries as not enough. Over the past generation, we have witnessed an attempt to change substantively the way American society is interpreted historically and presented artistically. Our times, in short, have produced a far more fervent call for a recasting of the interpretation of American culture and reforms in the way our diversified culture is supported. On college campuses across the nation, students and academicians have called for the dismantling of what is often called the Eurocentric approach to observing human activity. That challenge has taken on an acrimonious

> **The civil rights movement gave cultural pluralism a revitalized voice and a social, political and cultural agenda. The idea became more passionate, more distinctly ideological and, to some, more threatening.**

and political character. In the academic arena the challenge has brought curriculum reform and an attack on the traditional canon. It is strikingly reminiscent of the battles over ethnic and women's studies during the 1960s and early 1970s, in that the stakes are perceived to be high, the methods of attack and counterattack are often embittered, and civility is threatened.

Changes in American academic and artistic circles especially reflected the entrance of members of new ethnic groups and the descendants of American slaves into these professions. These new scholars and artists often questioned both the traditional consensus on American history and culture and the propriety of ethnic assimilation. Indeed, by the early 1970s, there was a broad criticism of all assimilationist theories and social strategies, especially the venerable American Melting Pot. When ethnic scholars carefully examined the idea of the Melting Pot, many argued that it was a seriously flawed ideal, in fact, a dangerous prospect for those groups which saw in their distinctiveness something of value and deserving of preservation. In one of the major critiques of the Melting Pot, Nathan Glazer and Daniel Patrick Moynihan wrote in 1963, "The initial notion of an American Melting Pot did not, it seems, quite grasp what would happen in America. At least it did not grasp what would happen in America in the short run, and since this short run encompasses at least the length of a normal lifetime, it is not something we can ignore." Moreover, they argue, "there is satisfaction in being with those who are like oneself. The ethnic group is something of an extended family or tribe. And aside from ties of feeling and interest, there are concrete ties of organization. Certain types of immigrant social organization have declined, but others have been as ingenious in remolding and recreating themselves as the group itself." That line of reasoning was embodied in the rhetoric of third-generation ethnic whites and, more stridently, among Native Americans, Afro-American cultural nationalists, Latinos and various Asian groups.

The critique of the American Melting Pot unleashed intense passions against other consensus views of American life during the 1960s. Discussions of what American culture had been, what it had become, increasingly threatened cross-cultural empathy. During the 1980s, a new generation of cultural pluralists in the academy and in arts and humanities institutions railed against Eurocentrism as a preservation ethic of Western culture that arguably has defined the debate on all other cultures. Those who took on the mantle of Western civilization were seen by more militant ideological cultural pluralists as blindly committed to a distorted and patriotic view of Euro-American history and contemporary life. Moreover, in what seemed to many a contradiction of traditional assimilationist objectives by the nation's largest ethnic groups, there was a call for various ethnocentric initiatives in the academy.

Not surprisingly, those who honor Western civilization have counterattacked, sometimes brilliantly. Cultural pluralism, recently known as *multiculturalism*, is disparaged as a divisive movement inspired by narrow political objectives. Advocacy for cultural diversity is seen as an invitation to a "new tribalism" in American life. Indeed, some of the nation's leading conservative and liberal thinkers foresee in cultural pluralism a pending apocalypse. Although pluralism is generally acknowledged as a prominent feature of American life, many conservatives and liberals oppose its concrete manifestations in important vectors of American life.

The swirling debate about the history of American culture and its present character is unlike anything in American life since the early years of the civil rights movement. It is a true test of the persistence of all sides.

♦ ♦ ♦ ♦

Many of the arguments concerning contemporary cultural matters have one weakness, at least: the contention that we Americans—blacks, browns, coloreds and whites—form solid, virtually self-contained blocs; that members of America's racial and ethnic groups have held, and continue to hold, thoughts and prejudices specifically related to their membership in a particular group, and that they have also taken, and continue to take, actions specifically related to their membership in the group. In one of the more recent popular polemics of race in American life, professor Shelby Steele sheds some light on this great flaw in the way we Americans view ourselves. He argues, for example, that many white and black Americans are now locked in a bitter battle over their respective roles in our current racial dilemma. Whites, he believes, simply want a restoration of their innocence from the ugly episodes of the past; they want the slate wiped clean and the business of promoting social harmony and equality to begin anew. In contrast, blacks, according to professor Steele, still cling to the memory of their difficult past and, bereft of real political and economic clout, have made it into an effective weapon against the majority population. They manipulate its

> **The swirling debate about the history of American culture and its present character is unlike anything in American life since the early years of the civil rights movement.**

**Armistice Day, November 11, 1918, at the Four
Corners in Newark, New Jersey**

powers through an appeal to a superior morality which victims
of the past can claim. Steele calls for a restoration of the importance of individual responsibility within the society and a cessa-
tion of aggregate group racial tactics.

But is it really fair to say that whites, blacks and other
ethnic minorities of color can be so easily generalized? Do not
class, generation, region, gender, individual taste and global
changes militate against the centrality of the group experience?

Do not these and other factors influence the intensity of group identification? They probably do. Yet the current debate over cultural pluralism often obscures the deepening complexity and fragmentation of the American cultural landscape.

Moreover, it would seem that the current emphasis on multiculturalism is actually promoting the old, and largely discredited, line of cultural exclusion. In becoming more concerned about cultural issues, many Americans have become more concerned about their own culture and its competitiveness with others, rather than about how we have all become more or less outsiders, or marginalized, in a fragmented society. This tendency toward reducing multiculturalism to a perception of monolithic behavior by particular groups will lead to group and individual frustration. Ethnic group leaders, perceiving their group as a monolith,

> **In becoming more concerned about cultural issues, many Americans have become more concerned about their own culture and its competitiveness with others, rather than about how we have all become more or less outsiders, or marginalized, in a fragmented society.**

will probably continue to use victimization as a means to advance their group, even in the face of increasing fragmentation of the group due to upward mobility, suburbanization, international contact, intermarriage and mass culture. And those who perceive themselves simply as whites will come to see cultural pluralism as a minority concern of blacks, Latinos, Native Americans and Asians. Real interest in multiculturalism may indeed wane as it is associated with being simply another minority issue, without broad support in American life.

In the chapters that follow, these concerns are explored through a discussion of the interrelationship of history, culture, art and arts policy in contemporary American life. Needless to say, cultural pluralism, as a vehicle by which these concerns can be discussed, has emerged as the dominant issue facing a wide swath of the American populace. Yet, its popularity and the integrity of the debate it has engendered are threat-

Exercise class for United Shoe Machinery Company employees, March 1913.

ened by the current economic crisis facing the United States. Because there are fewer dollars with which to reconcile the past inequities found in the arts, it is important to establish quickly a meaningful and issue-related approach to the challenge of arts access, support and appreciation facing many Americans.

2

The Troubled
Ascent of Modern
American Culture

T he origin of the current conflict over the proper role
and future of pluralism in American society and culture is much in doubt. Did it begin, as some have argued, during the twilight of the civil rights movement, when
black power advocates, in their broad and unrelenting attack
against white racism, caused many admirers of Western civilization to shudder as if their lives were threatened? Or are its ori-
gins to be found in the recent past, during the 1980s, with the
rising popularity of conservative crusades such as returning
prayer to public schools and overturning the Supreme Court's
1972 decision in *Roe v. Wade*? Perhaps its beginnings are to be
found on the bloody ground left by those New Yorkers who recently produced the much debated, if rarely read, *A Curriculum of
Inclusion: Report of the Commissioner's Task Force on Minorities.*

And did the conflict intensify when one of the nation's preeminent scholars, Arthur Schlesinger, broke ranks with many liberals and claimed that contemporary advocates of pluralism threatened to disunite the society?

The ferocity of what has come to be called *the culture wars* and the youthfulness of some of its combatants may contribute to the impression that cultural pluralism is a new idea having all of the provocative and precarious qualities of an unexplored intellectual territory. But that impression is not informed by history. As noted in the introductory chapter, cultural pluralism has been articulated by Americans since the early nineteenth century. It became an important feature of those ideals that formed the American creed. Indeed, not until the early twentieth century, when immigration threatened the nation's homogeneity, was America's often articulated reverence for diversity challenged by fears of disunity.

But if cultural pluralism is not new, why is it so wearisomely controversial today? Why the hard-edged rhetoric by those who oppose it as well as those who advocate it?

What is new about cultural pluralism, particularly in the way the idea intersects with the arts and the humanities, is the fragmentation of its proponents. There has, of course, long been disagreement between pluralists on matters having to do with race, nationality and political expressions, but not on the same scale as today. Some cultural pluralists are essentially ethnocentrists, whose primary objective is the advancement of their group's visibility and power in the society. Other pluralists are cultural liberals who envision an American cultural mosaic unified by commonly held ideals of participatory democracy, tolerance and progress for all. And there are those for whom America is to be likened to a tent that contains an array of distinct cultural blocs, "each with its own norm, beliefs, behaviors, attitudes, etc." Yet another variant on cultural pluralism is articulated by those who refer to "the shared experiences and co-existence of several different races and ethnicities." More recently, cultural pluralism has been used to describe efforts by other groups not necessarily racial or ethnic in character,

What is new about cultural pluralism, particularly in the way the idea intersects with the arts and the humanities, is the fragmentation of its proponents.

such as the physically challenged, gays, lesbians and bisexuals. Because of these varied persuasions, cultural pluralism is at once a syncretic term and an intellectual movement that means different things to different individuals and groups.

Long before the credo of cultural pluralism became a disparate movement, it appeared as a potentially divisive issue in modern American life. During the early twentieth century, roughly between 1900 and 1930, the great American scholars and founding fathers of modern cultural pluralism Horace Kallen and W.E.B. DuBois first sought a symmetry between the nation's differences and its sameness. But few endorsed their vision of a pluralistic cultural democracy. Indeed, American life at that time was sharply divided by a rigid color line in economic, social and cultural affairs. Attempts to enhance an appreciation of cultural difference were often met with extraordinary reaction. In an important study, the historian Rayford Logan argues that the early twentieth century was the nadir of the nation's race relations, years that were especially harmful to the aspirations of black Americans. Even from the considerable

Southern black migrants to Newark, New Jersey, 1918.

distance of our times, black Americans have much reason to denounce loudly their relegation to the bottom of American life at a time when so many newly arrived European immigrants were passing them by, politically and economically and in artistic recognition.

Notwithstanding the enormous difficulties faced by the forebears of contemporary pluralism, modern life made possible new views on race and culture. Demographic growth, spurred by European immigration and the migration of southern blacks to northern cities, and an enhanced understanding of the past by academically trained social and behavioral scientists encouraged progressive views of the cultures of all Americans, new and old.

The New Negroes of the Jazz Age, that is, those who settled urban centers in search of improved educational and economic opportunity, were among the first modernists to question the nation's preoccupation with Eurocentric ideas of culture. They were the intellectual mentors of many of today's cultural pluralists, the first dark Americans to redefine not only their own lives but as well the life of the larger, white society. Significantly, the ascent of that first generation of black modernists would symbolize a problematic feature of the cultural pluralist movement in the United States: its leadership by individuals of African ancestry. Indeed, because of the dark hue of its leading intellectual proponents and their criticism of Euro-American hegemony over historical interpretation, education and the arts, cultural pluralism has from the beginning of this century been viewed with considerable suspicion. New Negro artists and intellectuals, such as Alaine Locke, Langston Hughes, Zora Neale Hurston and DuBois, among several others, claimed that black culture embodied what was truly unique in American culture—its musical genius, its sense of rhythm, its humor, its pathos and, perhaps, its destiny. In a sense, blacks and other dark minorities articulated a new view of American culture because the emerging modern order required people with requisite skills and talents, attributes that over time became as important as wealth and breeding. In short,

> **The New Negroes of the Jazz Age were the intellectual mentors of many of today's cultural pluralists, the first dark Americans to redefine not only their own lives but as well the life of the larger, white society.**

"Radio Listening at Home," ca. 1929.

modern life enabled a more diversified group of Americans to interact with the larger society and insist upon better treatment.

Enlightened views on race and ethnicity, however, did not lead directly to a fundamental change in the social status of blacks and other dark ethnic groups; rather these views encouraged a broader discourse on culture that continues to captivate our attention. Many early-twentieth-century white Protestant Americans clung to an atavistic notion of race as they sought to ensure that racial customs in the society were never to change in ways that would imperil the importance and dominance of Anglo-American culture.

♦ ♦ ♦ ♦

The nation's great arts institutions emerged during this period, when art and culture were being viewed differently and when America became increasingly interested in its own native creativity. Those institutions, especially museums, were seeking to reconcile the obvious conflict between American democratic ideals and practice. During the early twentieth century, as Calvin Tomkins argues in his history of the Metropolitan Museum of Art, American museums were, on the one hand, "founded on the assumption that art was inseparable from education"; they "addressed their primary appeal to the man in the street." On the other hand, throughout their formative years—a period in which the narrow contours of American culture and art were being challenged by cultural pluralists— the leading museums resembled tightly knit social clubs. One of these, the Metropolitan Museum of Art, which had opened in 1880, was the recipient of especially harsh criticism, probably because, as the most prestigious art museum in the Western hemisphere, its elitism seemed to surpass that of all other museums. Collection building and exhibition policy in the nation's leading museums entailed, among other things, an acceptance of the growing power of a relatively new coterie of American urbanites—the so-called tastemakers, prosperous collectors and arts entrepreneurs. Their role in helping museums to acquire art, to cultivate powerful and affluent patrons, and to mount exhibitions can be easily criticized as an example of how the

> Many early-twentieth-century white Protestant Americans clung to an atavistic notion of race as they sought to ensure that racial customs in the society were never to change in ways that would imperil the importance and dominance of Anglo-American culture.

United States arts establishment, early in this century, ignored the ascendancy of different cultures and artistic expressions. Indeed, as John Cotton Dana observed in one of his typically shocking remarks, "No other public institutions give so little in return for the money spent on them as museums." Art museums, in his view, were devoted primarily to what he called the "cultured few." At the time Dana criticized museums' narrow view of their role in society, they were, in fact, facing important challenges to the traditional meaning of culture, challenges which portended the conflicts of our times.

The difficult adjustment of American museums to a pluralistic modern culture from the turn of the century until the post-World War II years actually reflected a broader uneasiness over the changes wrought by immigration, the great migration of blacks out of the South, urban development, racial progress and ethnic chauvinism. In a recent article on the emergence and importance of jazz in early-twentieth-century American culture, the historian Lawrence W. Levine examines how the evolution of the music both revealed the contemporary biases against indigenous American creativity and set the stage for a growing criticism against the Eurocentric dominance of American art. Until World War II, according to Levine, upwardly mobile white Americans saw culture as "traditional—the creation of centuries; it was harmonious, embodying order and reason." Significantly, during the 1920s Jazz Age, when artistic expression by blacks was flourishing, culture was seen as "exclusive, complex, available only through hard study and training." Jazz music, which for many white and black cosmopolitans was the most representative aspect of black creativity, also symbolized a radically different impulse in American society at a time when great American museums were becoming the quintessential cultural institutions in the society. They represented the preservation of highbrow culture in a society still uncertain of the integrity of its own national cultural identity. "Culture," Levine writes, "was the product of that side of ourselves that craved order, stability, definition. It was the expression of a colonial side of ourselves that we have not done nearly enough to understand. . . . Culturally we remained, to a much larger extent than we have

Romanian fortune telling booth at a fair, Mineola, Long Island, New York, 1932.

yet recognized, a colonized people attempting to define itself in the shadow of the former imperial power."

Because it threatened the old way of looking at culture and came from a group believed to be largely backward if not primitive, jazz was trivialized and denigrated. Similarly, the integrity of other artistic expressions by blacks was belittled by tastemakers, most of whom were white. White cosmopolitans rarely associated black visual art with the underside of black life that had produced jazz; nonetheless, they questioned it as real art. The late Gary Reynolds, curator of painting and sculpture at the Newark Museum, argued that the reception given to black artists in the early twentieth century was often marked by condescension.

As the leading museums pursued their respective collection policies in the years between the Jazz Age and the post-World War II period, their cultural and racial elitism set the stage for an increasingly acrimonious debate over the appropriate role of artistic expressions by minorities in American life. Black artists were accorded some recognition within the collections of these institutions, but it was never commensurate with their talent or their emerging numbers. Throughout the postwar period, black artists used *tokenism*—a word that had surfaced earlier in the racially stratified labor market—to describe their dilemma with museums. Their underrepresentation, we now know, was a corollary of the more fundamental problem of racial prejudice against blacks and other dark minority groups in art schools, in touring exhibitions and within the professional staffs of major museums.

Over time, what had been couched, quite incorrectly, as artistic issues involving blacks, Asians, Latinos, Native Ameri-

**Eddie "Rochester" Anderson with Veterans of
Foreign Wars at V.F.W. barbecue, Los Angeles, 1940.**

cans and other minorities were drawn into the passions of the
modern civil rights movement. As a result, the struggles over
artistic representation and validation increasingly became a
part of political discourse and the confrontational politics of the
1960s and 1970s. By 1968, in a scene reminiscent of the
"Don't Buy Where You Can't Work" campaigns waged by blacks
in northern cities during the 1930s, black artists and social ac-
tivists picketed an exhibition at the Whitney Museum of American Art. They assembled to protest the museum's exclusion of
works by black artists in a show that surveyed American art
produced during the 1930s. The demonstration raised the
specter that representation of the art produced by members

of minority groups would become a social issue wherein the importance of quality would be lost. By the 1970s, growing numbers of arts institutions, never fully confident that quality art could be found across the mosaic of cultures, succumbed to the pressure, especially when faced with the prospect of having their funds cut because of their racial insensitivity. Indeed, mainstream institutions did not revise their policies toward minorities until they were threatened with potentially embarrassing exposés of white racism. It may also be true that, as more minority arts institutions exhibited and developed their collections, the major museums, ever cognizant of competition, opened their doors to those traditionally kept out.

In the wake of the demonstrations at the Whitney, numerous attempts were made to shed light on black artistic expression. Those efforts came primarily through all-black shows at the nation's most prestigious museums and at traditionally black institutions. The Whitney mounted a massive exhibition in 1970; the Metropolitan Museum mounted its ambitious, if convoluted, "Harlem on My Mind" exhibition, which was followed by the New York Cultural Center's "Blacks USA: 1973" exhibition. Henri Ghent, formerly of the Brooklyn Museum, probably spoke for many pluralists when, in October 1973, he wrote in the *New York Times:*

> *Normally one would be extremely proud of these strides, perhaps even grateful, if these gestures of professional exposure (albeit involuntary) had produced the hoped for results: that* **quality** *black artists could enjoy participating in a kind of cultural democracy in the plastic arts, and could be exhibited alongside their white counterparts without the slightest consideration for ethnicity. However, with far too few exceptions, the "black" shows that have inundated us in*

*recent years can only be described as more token actions
taken by the arts establishment to relieve itself of the
mounting criticism from the black artistic community.*

The problem with the "black" art show syndrome of the
1970s and early 1980s was at once aesthetic, racial and political. In suggesting that work by black artists could be grouped,
organizers of such shows muted the particularity of art—the
voice of the artist. Moreover,
black shows seemed to some
a way of "Jim Crowing" the
black artist, reducing his or
her work to the racial back-
waters. If black artists are
to be grouped for racial reasons alone, it was reasoned,
their art is only of sociologi-
cal or political, not of artistic,
significance.

**By the 1970s, growing numbers
of arts institutions, never fully confident that quality art could be found
across the mosaic of cultures, succumbed to the pressure, especially
when faced with the prospect of having their funds cut because of their
racial insensitivity.**

Those issues, not surprisingly, created differences of opinion among blacks artists and within the museum world. In
early 1969, the *New York Times* reported artist Benny Andrews's
comment on the proliferation of exhibitions focusing exclusively
on work by black artists: "We're a trend like pop and op," he
said to *Times* reporter Grace Glueck. "We're the latest movement. Of course, like the others, we may be over in a year or
two." Other artists defended exhibitions by black artists as aes-
thetically sound. "I do think there is something found in the
works of the black artist that is absent in the art of other people," claimed the artist Hale Woodruff at a symposium sponsored by the Metropolitan Museum of Art. Others have claimed
that the intrinsic value of art from a historically oppressed people

should not lead to the clumsy categorizing of black art, which would be tantamount to ignoring the enormous differences that exist in this as in other forms of racial expression.

The concern over how best to bring cultural sensibilities in line with modern realities at American museums, symphony orchestras, and dance and theater companies raises at least two major questions. First, why has the dilemma of racial representation in contemporary artistic organizations remained so tenaciously a part of the arts establishment? Second, to what extent are arts professionals and scholars who are not members of a marginalized group qualified to interpret that group's experience, art and culture?

Duke Ellington, ca. 1970.

Regarding the first query, recent historical analysis of majority arts organizations has largely shown that, despite changes in other sectors of society, they remain bastions of social privilege and guardians of an ethos largely untouched by the varied intellectual and cultural nuances of darker ethnic groups. Historically, modern arts institutions have not been equipped structurally or programmatically to cope with the deep cultural tensions that accompany contemporary racial and cultural life. As one of many consequences of this limitation, major arts organizations have not figured out how to reconcile their ideals of ethnic inclusion with their traditions based upon a hierarchy for valuing artistic worth. It may be that the two are irreconcilable.

With respect to the second query, most arts professionals are far more informed about the nuances of different American cultural groups and their legitimate demands for greater access to recognition than was possible a generation ago. More than a generation after social and behavioral scientists' exploration of issues of marginality, many arts professionals have come to discover their own, as well as the interdependency of arts constituencies and human creativity. In the end, those who are entrusted with the task of explaining objects and images are increasingly less guided by their racial stock than by the seriousness with which they pursue their craft. Were that not the case, much of what we know about American culture would have been all the longer hidden behind the wall of racial and cultural segregation.

The current struggle over American culture, the culture wars, is in part a legacy of the way majority cultural institutions and spokespersons have underrepresented specific groups of Americans over the course of the twentieth century. The next chapter examines how this struggle has evolved, threatening to bring an ignoble end to the long search for American consensus amid difference.

3

The Current Debate

Many years of social, academic and arts activism have
taken their toll on the contemporary evolution of cultural pluralism in American life. What was once a
sharply focused, vital and largely optimistic vision of a
richly endowed cultural landscape has on some fronts,
especially in curriculum reform and the humanities, disin-
tegrated into a nasty and often uninformed fight over history, the meaning and the future of America. The struggle
has been fought most intensely by those who have considered the effect of demographic changes on the future political and cultural horizon of the United States. "Each year,"
Andrew Hacker writes, "this country becomes less white,
less 'European,' and less tightly bound by a single language. The United States now has a greater variety of

cultures than at any time in its history." Little wonder there is such debate over where we are going and how we should get there.

Since the early 1980s, the growing contest over the perception of what change has made of America has taken on powerfully ideological characteristics. Those calling for a fundamental reshaping of the nation's educational policies, the arts and other public enterprises, who may be called the *new cultural pluralists,* have argued that America does not have a common culture, that "the idea of 'mainstream American' is nothing more than an additional myth meant to maintain Eurocentric hegemony," according to Molefi Kete Asante, professor and chair of the Department of African American Studies at Temple University, and a leading advocate of Afrocentrism. Although the new cultural pluralists are differentiated ideologically and, not surprisingly, by sharp differences in personal style, they generally agree that there is a dire need to reconsider the development of American and world cultures from the vantage point of people of color and the victims of Western oppression. Or, as Amalia Mesa-Bains writes, "What we see in the African American, Latino, and certainly Asian American and Native American communities is a moving back toward the memory of origin."

> **W**hat was once a sharply focused, vital and largely optimistic vision of a richly endowed cultural landscape has on some fronts, especially in curriculum reform and the humanities, disintegrated into a nasty and often uninformed fight over history, the meaning and the future of America.

Theatre du Soleil's production of *The Libation Bearers*.

Over the past few years, the new cultural pluralists have faced a rising chorus of criticism, much of it from fellow academicians. They have been accused of promoting the balkanization of American life into self-contained cultural and ethnic blocs, of promoting a new tribalism in a nation traditionally in search of cultural and political consensus. Two important and widely read books by Allan Bloom and Roger Kimball deride multiculturalism as a threat to the traditional belief in an American cultural consensus and, more generally, to an appreciation of Western culture.

On this side of the battle line, there are those who may be called the *neoclassicists.* What is most striking about them is the essentially liberal character of their vision of American culture as cohesive and unified by commonly held values that transcend race, class and gender. Yet what we know most about the neoclassicists is what is said about them by others. Much like the new cultural pluralists, they are defined

> **Those calling for a fundamental reshaping of the nation's educational policies, the arts and other public enterprises . . . have argued that America does not have a common culture . . .**

as an opposition group. They are accused of membership in "the cultural right," of seeking to impose outmoded approaches to an understanding of history, culture and human potential; they are seen by their detractors as guardians of "white male Western culture," whose resistance to an expanded canon of books, ideas and precepts is an attempt to maintain the inequities of the past.

Although the subtle differences among the neoclassicists and new cultural pluralists are many, all combatants in the culture wars agree that the United States is rapidly becoming a new kind of society marked by unprecedented complexities in its many cultures. Hence, much of the current debate between the two groups centers on ways to discredit the other. Comparatively less attention is given to finding an appropriate balance or, better yet, a mutually beneficial reciprocity between the nation's various cultures.

The debate between neoclassicists and the new cultural pluralists has also ushered in a struggle over nomenclature. Although this monograph consistently uses the term *cultural pluralism,* many other names have been offered to denote the diverse quality of the American population and the diverse aspirations of its many cultural stocks. Included in this litany of nomenclatures are *cultural diversity, multiculturalism, transculturalism, ethnic pluralism* and *ethnic diversity* and, most recently, *cross-culturalism.*

Participant in children's activities at the Arts Festival of Atlanta.

It is important to recognize the legitimacy of each, but it is far more important to recognize them all as socially constructed terms that are designed to embody the complexity of a truly heterogeneous society. The varied nomenclatures of cultural pluralism are responsive primarily to current considerations of power relationships that are found in race, gender and class as well as to considerations of place and circumstance. Just as early-twentieth-century American intellectuals constructed the concept of cultural pluralism as an alternative to the Victorian penchant for order and structure imposed from the top, the racism directed against people of color, and the nativist reaction to poor European immigrants, our generation has redefined the issue to suit the far greater intricacies and group behaviors found in postmodern America.

The most obvious change in the construction of cultural pluralism is that for many it no longer bespeaks a celebration of the nation's diversity. Indeed, although cultural pluralism was once marked by a celebratory spirit, a call for intergroup tolerance and, alas, a naïveté toward the manifestations of economic power, the new cultural pluralism is far different. Thomas Sowell, senior fellow at the Hoover Institute on War, Revolution and Peace at Stanford University and a critic of the new cultural pluralism, claims that it often announces "a sweeping criticism of the United States, or even a condemnation of Western civilization as a whole." Because of this sharpened edge in the rhetoric of cultural pluralists, he calls for a separation of the general importance of cultural diversity from "the more specific, more parochial, and more ideological agendas that have become associated with this word in recent years." Sowell also seems to think that proponents of the new cultural pluralism have become zealots at heart, unfazed by the complexity of their doctrine and the consequences of their activities in the culture wars.

Sowell, along with other critics of cultural pluralism, reserves his sharpest criticism for a relatively new form of cultural pluralism, a hard-edged *monoculturalism* or *ethnocentrism.* That perspective, as historian Thomas Bender recently observed, is characterized by a belief that culture is "tightly bounded, self-contained, pure, and fixed."

In a far-ranging critique of this new variant of cultural pluralism, the historian Arthur Schlesinger argues that it has all but disassociated itself from traditional approaches to promoting diversity in the United States. "The ethnic upsurge (it can hardly be called a revival because it was unprecedented) began as a gesture of protest against the Anglocentric culture. It became a cult, and today it threatens to become a counter-revolution against the original theory of America as one people, a common culture, a single nation." Schlesinger further argues:

> *The ethnicity rage in general and Afrocentricity in particular not only divert attention from the real needs but exacerbate the problems. The recent apotheosis for ethnicity, black, brown, red, yellow, white, has revived the dismal prospect that in happy melting-pot days, Americans thought the republic was moving safely beyond—that is, a society fragmented into separate ethnic communities. The cult of ethnicity exaggerates differences, intensifies resentments and antagonisms, drives ever deeper the awful wedges between races and nationalities. The endgame is self-pity and self-ghettoization.*

When a liberal scholar as widely respected as Professor Schlesinger weighs in against the quintessential liberal idea of cultural diversity, it is probably a good sign that we should

Blues Week concert on the campus of Davis and Elkins College, Elkins, West Virginia, 1992.

take notice of what has become of the consensus that diversity is a benefit in the American commonweal. Most critics of cultural pluralism claim that it has gone astray in recent years, that it has lost its moorings and become a disguise for ideological attacks against Western civilization and whites. They argue that the moral absolutist stance of the new cultural pluralists ignores one of the most important qualities of Western civilization: its willingness to right the wrongs committed against people of color, dependent social classes, and women—in short, its penchant for democratic rights. "The Western tradition," Schlesinger and the historian Diane Ravitch observe, "is the source of ideas of individual freedom and political democracy to which most of the world now aspires. . . . This philosophy has included and empowered people of all nations and races."

The most important recent source for the animus directed against the new cultural pluralism is found in the efforts by school systems to incorporate multiculturalism in social studies and humanities curricula. More specifically, the battle lines were drawn soon after the implementation of the African American Baseline Essays in the Portland, Oregon, school district and the later release of *A Curriculum of Inclusion,* which was completed in New York in 1987. In both cases, pluralists advocated an

Most critics of cultural pluralism claim that it has gone astray in recent years, that it has lost its moorings and become a disguise for ideological attacks against Western civilization and whites.

Afrocentric approach to learning, and local racial politics intersected with revisionist interpretations of history and culture. In an article detailing her experiences as a consultant with the New York initiative in multiculturalism, Ravitch recalls that the curriculum submitted by the "committee on minorities" was antiwhite and antiwestern in tone and that it would "not advance the cause of multiculturalism."

Not only is it likely that *A Curriculum of Inclusion* has weakened support for multiculturalism, as Ravitch warns, but it has also provoked a further fragmentation in the ranks of cultural pluralists. Ravitch, for example, published several articles in *The American Educator, American Scholar* and *Contention* critical of *A Curriculum of Inclusion* and other educational initiatives influenced by Afrocentrism. Like many who have criticized Afrocentrism, she argues it is not a variant of cultural pluralism:

> *I believe that it is a repudiation of multiculturalism. In my view, multiculturalism is both a field of study that examines the interaction of diverse people and a condition in society that results when different cultures mix and mingle and interact. Segregation of, or separatism by, any group is not multicultural; Afrocentrism is a sort of intellectual apartheid, and as such it is the antithesis of multiculturalism.*

In an earlier work, Ravitch argues that multiculturalism has been weakened by the extremism of the new cultural pluralists, some of whom, she claims correctly, are particularists because their focus is on their group, not on the larger and far more complicated mosaic of cultures that now make up American society. "Today, pluralistic multiculturalism must contend with a new, particularist multiculturalism," she writes. "The pluralists seek a richer common culture; the particularists insist that no common culture is possible or desirable."

Another important criticism of the Afrocentric variant of cultural pluralism comes from the historian Gary B. Nash. Nash laments the many years of invisibility imposed on the history and culture of racial minorities in the United States and criticizes the shoddy scholarship that characterized early-twentieth-century academicians and the virulent anti-intellectualism of some of the neoclassicists (in particular, Dinesh D'Souza, the

Okinawan Dance, Majikina Honryu Buyo Dojo.

author of *Illiberal Education: The Politics of Race and Sex on Campus*). However, he takes issue with the more militant form of Afrocentrism found in the writings and speeches of Professors Molefi Kete Asante, Leonard Jeffries and Asa Halliard, and the community-based educator Wade Nobles. Nash fears that Afrocentrism, which he correctly argues has much deeper historical roots than are generally recognized, has in recent years evolved into a particularist ideology that promotes the kind of racist logic its proponents ardently denounce. It is, he maintains, a romantic fantasy in search of a broadly based reassessment of the role of Africa in the development of Western civilizations.

> *The non-scholarly form of Afrocentrism, drawing on a long-established movement to stop measuring all things by the European cultural yardstick, has moved perilously close to holding up a new yardstick which measures all things by how nearly they approach an African ideal. When we get beyond levels and cultural yardstick waving, what will be enduringly important for those who wish to study the interaction of African peoples and Europeans, in whatever part of the world, is an ability to look through several sets of lenses. Most of us learned a long time ago that this was what good history and good anthropology are all about. It is hardly arguable that to understand African literature or African American history or Afro-Brazilian music one must have understanding of African culture as well as the cultures with which Africans were interacting. Nor is it deniable that the stigmatizing of African culture and its derivative cultures of the diaspora has been an essential part of white supremacist thought and that it has been institutionalized in our culture and in the culture of all societies where Europeans were the cultural arbiters. But Afrocentrism becomes a new and dangerous ethnocentrism of its own when it adopts the colonizers' old trick of arranging cultures on a continuum ranging from inferior to superior.*

Much of the debate over cultural pluralism is found among academicians, particularly social scientists and humanists. There is also a wealth of writing and speaking by those interested in public education. To be sure, the culture wars are being fought mainly over the future of the American classroom and the texts and pedagogical sensibilities that will ultimately be used there. Not unlike neoclassicists, the new cultural pluralists, particularly those who are ethnocentrists, have largely contributed to the swirling debate over history, cultural matters and public policy in their writings, speeches and conferences. In short, most are men and women of letters. One of the leading figures, Molefi Kete Asante, is extremely persuasive because he realizes that considerable blame for the tragedies and inequities of the past and present can be placed upon white

Wynton Marsalis at a "Jazz for Young People" concert, Lincoln Center, New York, 1992.

society and modern defenders of Western civilization through ethno-nationalistic appeals for separation and self-determination. Afrocentricity, according to this line of reasoning, means "literally placing African ideals at the center of any analysis that involves African culture and behavior." Equally important, Asante and other Afrocentrists realize that the contemporary parlance of American culture is riddled with racially biased meanings that shape virtually all discussions regarding American culture. Asante's disparagement of the concept of "mainstream" American culture is important because it reveals an important aspect of ethnocentrism: its attempt to bring into question the centrality of Western-oriented symbols long considered sacrosanct. Afrocentrists are consistent in their rejection of the language of traditional American pluralism. "There is no common American culture as is claimed by the defenders of the status quo," Asante observes. Further, he argues that some pluralists (e.g., those who would side with Ravitch) are actually in support of a "hegemonic culture" dominated by values unique to Western civilization.

◆ ◆ ◆ ◆

With such posturing over the epistemology and direction of cultural pluralism, it is important to keep in mind that concern over the patrimony of American culture is not new. The anxieties of the present, like those of the past, are attributable largely to dramatic demographic changes in the United States. Since the 1965 enactment of an immigration reform law, which ended decades of preference to immigrants from western Europe, the number of foreign-born in the population dramatically increased—to 13.2 percent in 1980, the highest in the past 30 years. The influx has been mainly from the Third World

Tony West and the Imani Dancers.

nations, from China, Cuba, the Dominican Republic, India, Mexico, the Philippines and Vietnam.

This newest immigration, however, comes at a time when pluralism, as Americans have traditionally known it, has lost its appeal for most ethnic groups, with the exception of Afro-Americans, Latinos and the newest immigrants from Asia, Africa and the Caribbean. In his recently published book *Ethnic Identity: The Transformation of White America,* Richard D. Alba finds that ethnic identity was extremely weak among the "ethnic" whites whose forebears came to the United States in the late nineteenth and early twentieth centuries. In the critical areas by which ethnic consciousness can be measured—residential concentration, business development, discrimination, cuisine, attachment to an ancestral home, ethnic organizational membership and marriage—Alba found that white ethnics are ethnic in name only. Ethnicity, once thought to be exclusive, seems to have become inclusive. What seems to distinguish these "ethnics" is their recognition of European ancestry or, to put it bluntly, their whiteness.

Another study on the new white ethnicity, by Mary C. Waters, draws many of the same conclusions as Alba does. Ethnicity among white Americans, she argues, has acquired many of the characteristics of a commodity. For many white Americans "ethnicity is increasingly a personal choice of whether to be ethnic at all, and, for an increasing majority of people, of which ethnicity to be."

The reaction against the more virulent forms of cultural pluralism—Afro, Latino and Eurocentrism—should not, however, obscure their considerable influence in contemporary American life. The movement is far from dead, although it has been weakened by persistent criticisms from conservatives and liberals. Since the 1960s, when academic presses throughout the nation began to publish important texts in Afro-American history and Black Studies, cultural pluralism in its various forms has attracted some of the nation's leading scholars. And there have also been far more books dealing with the role and identity of women in society.

◆ ◆ ◆ ◆

As the culture wars continue to rage, a growing number of publications have surfaced on the role of the arts in an increasingly diverse American culture. Most of the existing literature explores ways to ensure equity in the appreciation, presentation and funding of the arts. In short, arts interests seem to be far more concerned with finding practical solutions to blatant inequities than with fundamentally restructuring the arts hierarchy. This work, some of which is very good, has been in response to the encouragement of the National Endowment for the Arts (NEA) and the National Endowment

> **Arts interests seem to be far more concerned with finding practical solutions to blatant inequities than with fundamentally restructuring the arts hierarchy.**

for the Humanities (NEH), both of which have urged the field to broaden constituency and genre, and, in effect, to democratize their operations. There has also been a proliferation of forums, workshops and professional conferences that seek to sensitize arts professionals to the exigencies of cultural pluralism and to serve as vehicles for discussions between cultural pluralists and arts professionals.

Considerably less attention has been devoted to increasing an understanding of the interrelationship between the arts and recent changes in demography and American conceptions of culture and history. One of the more ambitious efforts to encourage a broader and more critical conceptualization of American culture and the arts was made in 1989 by the Forum on the American Aesthetic, which served as the centerpiece of the humanities component of the California-based Festival 2000. Its objective was to "1) initiate a framework for a new body of critical thinking, 2) propel the creation of a new vocabulary for the development of critical writing and evaluation, and 3) encourage new partnerships which integrate multicultural traditions and contemporary ways of thinking in order to more effectively explore the issues of culture being greater than art and the impact of all cultures on the American aesthetic."

Spiderwoman Theater's production of *Power Pipes.*

Despite the paucity of critical literature on cultural plural-ism in the arts, the debate over its value and meaning follows, as in educational reform and the humanities, two distinct lines of reasoning. Some have attacked the new cultural pluralism as an affront to cultural and artistic values most Americans have long held dear. In a recent issue of the influential arts journal *The New Criterion*, editor Hilton Kramer takes a broad swipe at the cultural pluralist movement:

> *In the course of the last decade this cultural revolution has acquired new labels and new agendas, of which the move-ment that goes by the name of "multiculturalism" is no doubt the most capacious and the most lethal, but the essential lineaments of this revolutionary impulse have been apparent for some years now, and so have been its disastrous effects on education, on the arts and humanities, and on the entire tenor of moral debate and political argument in our society. It is a cultural revolution that has succeeded in making race, gender, and class the touchstones governing every question that concerns the life and thought of the nation, which means that it has succeeded in undermining the very principles upon which our nation was founded.*

The new cultural pluralists claim that the clamor over quality and standards is a smoke screen that seeks to disguise the hegemonic ten-dencies of Western cultures.

Howard Risatti, editor of the *New Art Examiner*, takes a somewhat different approach but reaches similar conclusions. He argues that the concerns of the new cultural pluralists, many of whom have been influenced by the theory of cultural relativ-ism, have led "to a more extremist position" wherein the idea of quality in Western visual art is being questioned, despite the prevalence of high standards and connoisseurship in much of non-Western artistry. Moreover, in their attacks against a tradition of Western "oppression," the new cultural pluralists have disregarded the facts of its counterparts in other cultures. "For sad as it is," Risatti writes, "history shows that inhumanity has no ethnic, cultural, geographic, or temporal limits."

Not unlike the debate over curriculum issues, the insistence on artistic quality has become a major issue in cultural pluralism. Neoclassicists generally criticize what they perceive to be the devolution of standards by artists and the organizations and institutions that present their work. Roger Kimball, writing in *The New Criterion*, argues, for example, that

> *Fashionable artists and critics are drifting farther and farther from any contact with the realm of aesthetic experience, which—despite the noisy cultural vicissitudes and depredations of the Eighties—remains the true source of arts and the gravamen of criticism. What the artists and writers—and increasingly, alas, the public as well—are left with are series of objects that range from the trivial to the repulsive, accompanied by endless commentaries that present a variety of tried and true political slogans in as pretentious a manner as possible.*

This view, not surprisingly, has not gone unchallenged. The new cultural pluralists claim that the clamor over quality and standards is a smoke screen that seeks to disguise the hegemonic tendencies of Western cultures. "Bourgeois hegemonic culture," Benjamin H.D. Buchloh observes, "has always used the tool of 'quality' to make other cultural practices marginal."

♦ ♦ ♦ ♦

Cultural pluralism and the culture wars of which it is a part have left us with much to consider about change in America, but little on which to agree. The language of cultural pluralism has become a blur of words that are often used with imprecision, such as *culture* and *society*. Moreover, its supporting vocabulary is without a consensus. But perhaps the greatest difficulty in making sense of the culture wars is the deepening cleavage between

Historian Thomas Bender calls for a negotiated public culture that is at once embracing of all cultures and devoted to what he calls a workable principle of synthesis.

its combatants. Neoclassicists are criticized for their allegedly arrogant allegiance to European hegemony in a society of settlers largely from the Third World. Concomitantly, the new cultural pluralists, especially those who adhere to an ethnocentrist approach to education, history, culture and the arts, are criticized for their anti-intellectualism and racist views of whites. As a result, much of the current literature and discussion about cultural pluralism is characterized by a lack of scholarly detachment and civility, evidenced in the controversial speeches of leading Afrocentrists, neoclassicists, feminists and Marxists.

Arts interests may indeed rise above the culture wars, but they will have to learn from what has become of cultural pluralism as both an intellectual and a political movement. In a thoughtful treatise, the historian Thomas Bender calls for a negotiated public culture that is at once embracing of all cultures and devoted to what he calls a workable principle of synthesis. Bender is right when he suggests that all discussions of culture in postmodern America are now shaped by the global scale of culture, the inability of any cultural voice to have hegemonic powers and the inevitable desire by historically marginalized groups to "enter the world of global culture making." Further, he argues:

> In our writing and our teaching, we can begin to move to a notion of a national synthesis but with "nation" understood in a new way. It is not a fixed container into which everything and everyone must be fitted; rather, it is an ever-changing, always contingent outcome of a contest among traditions, ideas, and social groups for the power to define public culture.

This is a paradigm worthy of further consideration by all combatants in the culture wars and, as argued in the final chapter, an especially fortuitous objective for those who serve American creativity.

4

Pragmatism and Idealism in the Culture Wars

A s the sometimes acrimonious and increasingly lively debate over cultural pluralism in the arts continues to unfold, we might consider its likely direction. Obviously, the sheer energy with which pluralists and their adversaries make their arguments will undoubtedly exhaust both camps within a few years. Throughout American history there is ample evidence that Americans soon tire of dilemmas for which there are no easy solutions. I suspect, too, that we may soon tire of multiculturalism.

Perhaps the greatest dilemma facing the future of cultural pluralism is that it has sought to embrace an agenda that is at once too broad and contradictory. While cultural pluralism during the early twentieth century was reasonably successful in

***Stepping into Ancient Egypt: The House of the Artist Pashed*, Newark Museum Junior Gallery, Newark, New Jersey.**

constructing new ways to perceive the value of diversity in the United States, the current permutation is having great difficulty because of the uncomfortable relationship between race and ethnicity. As Alan Wolfe persuasively argues, "At the very time when white ethnics are discovering that their historical identities are less distinctive, racial minorities are insisting on their racial differences. Much of the tension that characterizes contemporary debates over multiculturalism and diversity may be due to this contrasting trajectory." White ethnics, no longer clinging to Old World identities, and deeply influenced by mass commodity culture, are unlikely to support special initiatives in diversity, particularly in education. Their opposition may be as much racially motivated as it is a consequence of their assimilation in the anonymous white mainstream, where uniqueness is simply not promoted or desirable.

A similarly uncomfortable relationship currently exists between visions of a pluralistic culture and the problems arising from class differences and conflict. Modern America, much to its discredit, has kept staggering numbers of blacks and browns trapped in poverty and ignorance. The disparity between people of color and whites, which has long been a feature of our society and is now widening, powerfully infuses race into discussions about culture and art. Race, in short, overrides class in

> **A**ttempts to create a mosaic of relatively equal cultures are ... made all the more difficult because beneath the veneer of intergroup harmony there is ... the frightening prospect of socio-racial catastrophe.

American life, leading inevitably to an indifference to the effects of social deprivation on ethnic consciousness and culture. Attempts to create a mosaic of relatively equal cultures are then made all the more difficult because beneath the veneer of intergroup harmony there is, as was seen recently in the Los Angeles riots, the frightening prospect of socio-racial catastrophe.

Moreover, the debate over cultural pluralism, not unlike earlier ideological tussles, will dissipate as large public and private institutions respond to the most egregious insults to cultural democracy. It is simply not in the best interest of modern institutions, whether they are public or private, to be blatantly exclusionary. As the civil rights movement proved more than a generation ago, segregation and other forms of injustice are injurious to business. In this sense, modern America has something in common with the early American life—pragmatism and accommodation.

Urban Bush Women's production of *Praise House*.

Yet the near future must not be seen as, or allowed to become, simply a holding pattern. The continued general decline in adequate arts funding, the threats to artistic freedom and the muted appreciation of the cultivated arts by ethnic minorities demand that an affirmative response be taken by arts leaders. One possible scenario which could follow from inactivity in the culture wars is that the arts will continue to be perceived as an elitist pursuit, irrelevant to the interests and needs of the majority of the American people. Indeed, the former Republican presidential candidate Patrick J. Buchanan, hardly a friend to the ideals of pluralism, has called the National Endowment for the Arts "the upholstered playpen of the arts and crafts auxiliary of the Eastern liberal establishment." Mr. Buchanan's neoconservative attack on the arts in America, though offensive and shocking, could nonetheless find support among ethnic Americans who, despite their opposition to his other positions, may give comfort to his attack on the arts because they perceive that the arts serve only affluent white Americans.

◆ ◆ ◆ ◆

This study shows there is a need for arts leaders and the institutions they represent to become actively involved in shaping the future relationship between arts interests that represent culturally specific groups and those that represent a centrist view of Euro-American culture. Inasmuch as these interests will continue to face off over the issues of funding, aesthetic values (quality and interpretation) and power in the near future, there is a need to create a forum for productive discussion, problem solving and the creation of a common agenda. Arts interests across the cultural spectrum should be challenged to reach a consensus on the appropriate language for meaningful discussions on diversity. Participants in the culture wars often choose language as their battleground. The nomenclatures used to describe varying visions of history, art and culture are not clearly drawn or defensible. Moreover, they are often poorly presented in public rhetoric, position papers and bureaucratic documents. Imprecise language is, or at least should be, an anathema to artistically informed individuals. However, since there have been significant changes in American culture and artistic expressions since World War II, the language used to discuss the arts is often vague and counterproductive to real communication between combatants in the culture wars. Hence, a better, perhaps revised, understanding of the epistemology of culture and the etymology of cultural groups is desperately needed.

There is also considerable confusion over what might be called the symbolic features of ethnic and cultural protests in modern America. During the 1960s, for example, many Americans envisioned black power as a radical threat to the nation. In fact, it was a corollary of ethnic group mobility, remarkably similar to earlier efforts by European immigrants to control, to some extent, the leading institutions of their communities. Had there been greater understanding of traditional ethnic mobility strategies, the importance of racism in shaping the rhetoric of blacks during the 1960s, and ethnic symbolism (often found in language), black power could have had a better future. Such an effort could have been extremely valuable to improving the lives of black Americans and preserving the quality of American urban civilization. Although cultural pluralism has suffered from some of the prejudices directed against black power, it has the potential of inspiring a more enlightened response than was possible more than 20 years ago.

A Celebration with Celia Cruz, featuring Tito Puente and his Latin Jazz Orchestra, Lincoln Center, 1992.

Moreover, there is a need for leaders in the arts to promote policy initiatives that are informed by the conflicts that characterize the culture wars rather than by the illusion of a consensus which has rarely existed in American history. In most areas of the nation, public and private funding agencies and arts service organizations simply seek to do the right thing: they have encouraged the groups they support to seek broad access, broad representation and broad appeal. Though laudable, these objectives will, if continued, probably do little to change the way arts groups are funded and the way the arts are viewed by our fellow citizens. They actually represent an attempt to use liberal arts reform to preserve the status quo.

Arts policy in the United States is largely tied to habits that may have lost their relevance in a rapidly changing society. Among those traditions are: first, arts by discipline, which places a far greater value on European artistic forms than on those shaped by Asian, Pacific, African, Native American and Latino cultures; second, audience development, which generally encourages the darker members of the population to experience Eurocentric culture or, as is increasingly the case, non-European art in venues that have little role in ethnic communities, often called multicultural marketing; and third, the professionalization of arts interests, which over the past generation has created a network of relatively powerful arts constituencies that are represented by not-for-profit service organizations and are served, as it were, by state, regional and federal agencies. As a result of these habits, arts policy in the United States has come to favor what some cultural pluralists see as "an official culture" marked by its Eurocentric distinctiveness.

> **There is a need for leaders in the arts to promote policy initiatives that are informed by the conflicts that characterize the culture wars rather than by the illusion of a consensus which has rarely existed in American history.**

A pragmatic policy initiative in the arts that is informed by the reality of demographic change and the ideals inspired by cultural pluralism would seek to expand the arts arena by recruiting new arts interests that have been ignored. It would assume that, under present conditions, the arts are imperiled by the sheer numbers of Americans who have little understanding of where and how the arts can be appreciated. And it would seek to measure its success through a periodic evaluation of the accomplishment of its objectives.

Arts leaders and the institutions they serve should also consider the remarkable success of the popular arts over the past generation as a prototype for multicultural initiatives. Popular American music, for example, was segregated as recently as the 1950s, but as the potential mass market of consumers was identified, traditional categories were abandoned in favor of more inclusive categories of style and popular taste. Moreover, since World War II the traditional lines of separation between highbrow, middlebrow and lowbrow cultures have narrowed considerably. As Lawrence Levine observes, "Evidence of what appears to be a growing cultural eclecticism and flexibility is everywhere at hand." Perhaps through the collective leadership of service organizations, conservative arts interests and those who seek fundamental changes in the arts establishment will reconsider the existing divisions of art disciplines in light of contemporary realities—the crumbling of the American cultural hierarchy.

Challenging arts interests to use clearer and more communicable language about culture and the arts essentially calls for an intellectual exercise, one usually considered the province of academies of higher learning. But since colleges and universities cannot keep pace with the crisis of intercultural communication, the major arts service organizations should consider taking a leadership role in this area. Specifically, annual seminars on cultural diversity, which should be modeled upon the Aspen Institute for Humanistic Studies, could be presented. The objective of the seminars would be to bring together a diverse group of arts leaders in an intellectually

Newark Community School of the Arts, Newark, New Jersey.

exciting environment where the issue of diversity in the arts could be explored and critiqued.

Such seminars would help the arts in both tangible and intangible ways. They would presumably represent a major step beyond the current reliance on "one shot" conferences in which arts professionals recycle old agenda issues and redis- cover frustrations that have plagued cultural dialogue for many years. Ideally, major arts service organizations would pool their resources to publish annually occasional papers on diversity in the arts by leading behavioral scientists, humanists and arts leaders who participated in the seminars. Inasmuch as there is a lack of objective literature in this field, although an abundance exists in education and historical studies, such a publication, widely distributed, would use new scholarship on the arts to enhance understanding by arts professionals on the relationships that exist between race, class, gender and culture.

Developing policy initiatives informed by the current debate over diversity could take the form of establishing a policy center on diversity. The center should have its own staff and periodically involve former participants in the previously mentioned annual seminars on arts diversity and selected representatives from arts service organizations. Such organizations would include ACA, NEA, the National Assembly of State Arts Agencies (NASAA), the National Assembly of Local Arts Agencies (NALAA) and the Association of American Cultures (AAC), among others. By compiling quantitative data, collecting organizational and market studies and conducting its own surveys of the field, the center could critically examine the way diversity in the arts is currently supported and presented in the United States. It could also recommend to the field policies and strategies on various arts issues related to pluralism and the advancement of cultural democracy.

A reconsideration of the existing conceptualization of artistic fields in the light of significant changes in American society would entail an effort to bring together leaders in the arts with a wide array of leaders in popular culture, including film, television and theater producers, newspaper and magazine editors, sports figures, entertainment moguls, publishers and pollsters. Discussions among these leaders would aim at exploring (1) the relationship of popular culture to not-for-profit arts; (2) the dissemination of mass consumer culture across ethnic, racial and cultural lines; and (3) the ways in which the arts are produced and appreciated in our diversified society. The long-range purpose of such discussions would be to consider the relevance of popular or mass cultural dissemination (marketing and cross-fertilization of styles) to the not-for-profit arts scene.

Each of the aforementioned initiatives would obviously necessitate long-range planning and funding support before implementation. It is also clear that each may seem threatening to the existing arts bureaucracies because of the implicit assumption that pragmatic changes in the arts hierarchy are desperately needed if the arts are to remain a prominent feature in American life. Yet, since each initiative involves internal reform led by participants who have much to gain from change, arts leaders should be willing to help combatants in the culture wars reach a negotiated peace based upon mutual self-interest.

5

Parting Shots

Multiculturalism has gained a foothold in many areas of American life and culture. In art it is the recognition that each distinct community has its share of artists who reflect their culture's social and aesthetic values. No place better illustrates this than the Borough of Queens [New York] with its many communities representing over a hundred different languages and cultures.

T his excerpt from a 1992 newsletter of the Queens Museum of Art echoes sentiments favorable to tolerance and diversity found across the nation in public and private organizations and institutions. Pluralism has become one of the prominent symbols of our age; it now rivals an earlier generation's—Americans of the late nineteenth century—search for stability during a time of turbulent change.

This study has found that, despite the rancor and the drawn battle lines, few Americans dispute the value of pluralism. What we disagree on is the definition of the term and the direction in which pluralism may take us. Generally, the term has come to mean non-white and non-European; it is a euphemism for color-particular historical circumstances.

The available literature in the arts, though scant and superficial, reflects this bias. Rarely are European traditions and the artistic traditions usually ascribed to whites seen as culturally specific, although they are and always have been. Rarer still are references to the cross-fertilization of the world's cultures, despite solid evidence by more than a generation of scholarship that cultural groups always borrow and learn liberally from one another. In her recently published study of life in eighteenth-century

One gets the impression that the objective of cultural pluralism in the arts is not to recognize and further encourage the reciprocity and curiosity between various cultures and artistic expressions but, rather, to promote parity in funding.

Virginia, the historian Mechal Sobel writes, "Notwithstanding vast differences, both [Africans and English] brought preindustrial cultures to the New World in which there were far greater similarities with respect to modal attitudes and values than has generally been recognized. It was thus possible for many values and practices to meld or to reinforce one another, and this in fact did happen." Other studies in history, anthropology and cultural geography, among others, have shown culture to be organic and ever-changing in response to the present.

© David Lee

The Charles Moore Dance Company.

Yet, from my survey of current arts literature, it would seem that concerns over the future of America's cultures involve competing constituencies and financially driven reforms. Indeed, one gets the impression that the objective of cultural pluralism in the arts is not to recognize and further encourage the reciprocity and curiosity between various cultures and artistic expressions but, rather, to promote parity in funding. For example, in its 1989 "Report on Cultural Pluralism," the National Assembly of State Arts Agencies notes that indicators of accomplishment toward cultural diversity "can be examined with regard to *absolute numbers, dollar amounts, staff and council contact hours, per-cents* (of agency numbers, $, time) and *trends* pertaining to identified target groups." Financial parity, though essential for a truly pluralist arts arena, is hardly an appropriate first step toward an understanding of other cultures.

It would be far more useful to begin intercultural negotiations between a vast array of arts interests assembled in search of a recognition of both their differences and their sameness, of how social class now unites and divides individuals far more than culture does, and of how artistic endeavors long separated by tradi-

Puppet from Jusaburo Tsujimura's *Kecho*.

tion can be presented in new ways informed by contemporary realities of urban and rural geography. Thomas Bender, in a perceptive and hopeful call for synthesis in American historical scholarship, may have something of value for the 'arts when he observes, "The study of public culture is more than conventional political history. To describe the public culture of a society is to explain how power in all its various forms—including tradition itself—is contested, elaborated, and rendered authoritative. It also is about personal and collective self-identification." This view is complementary to that of educator Gerald Graff—in the absence of consensus, teach the conflicts!

If cultural pluralism is to succeed in the arts ... substantive changes will have to be made in the perception of cultural and artistic worth. Arts interests need to know, especially now, that cultural pluralism embodies bartering as a necessary, and even honorable, exercise among equals.

Arts policy in the United States has generally been shaped by an avoidance of negotiation amid conflict because arts interests have rarely had to talk directly to one another from positions of mutual respect. Divided by history and conflicting perceptions of their respective worth, arts interests remind one of the behavior of nation-states on the eve of great cataclysms of the twentieth century. If cultural pluralism is to succeed in the arts, as it appears to be succeeding in informing methodologies in the behavioral sciences, substantive changes will have to be made in the perception of cultural and artistic worth. Arts interests need to know, especially now, that cultural pluralism embodies bartering as a necessary, and even honorable, exercise among equals.

Glossary of Key Terms

A CURRICULUM OF INCLUSION

The title of the 1989 Report to the Commissioner of Education of New York State by the Task Force on Minorities: Equity and Excellence. The Report, which triggered a raging debate within the Task Force, documents the omission, distortions and untruths about the contributions of African Americans, Puerto Ricans/Latinos, Asian Americans and Native Americans to the history and development of the United States, as found in the curriculum syllabi of the New York State Education Department.

ACCULTURATION

The process whereby the members of one group adopt the customs of another.

AFROCENTRISM

A contemporary variant of earlier forms of African and African American nationalism, and a critical perspective that uses African rather than European ideals to study and appreciate African heritage. It purports to undermine prevailing beliefs about universal behavior and cultural standards.

AFFIRMATIVE ACTION

Compliance with and enforcement of legal requirements that prescribe specific goals, policies and practices deemed essential to addressing and correcting prior and traditional forms of institutional behavior and treatment which served to exclude people and organizations based on race.

CROSS-CULTURAL

The blending or incorporating of the cultural patrimony and/or nuances of one group with another or others. A contemporary variant on the cultural pluralism first called for in the early twentieth century which advocates great particularity among different cultural groups.

CULTURAL PLURALISM
(often used interchangeably with Cultural Diversity)

A term first coined in the early twentieth century by Horace M. Kallen which became a paradigm that recognizes the equal value, benefit, involvement and participation of various cultures in the general culture of a society.

CULTURE

In anthropology, the way of life of a society, a concept used to distinguish human societies from animal groups. Culture is formed from the customs, ideas and attitudes shared by a group and is transmitted from generation to generation by learning processes. The scientific use of the term, established in the late nineteenth century by Sir Edward Burnett Tylor, also took on adjectival characteristics, including high, low, highbrow, lowbrow and popular culture.

CUSTOM

A habitual group pattern of behavior that is transmitted from one generation to another, though not biologically; the core of human culture, especially in preindustrial and rural areas.

ETHNIC

A distinct category within the population of a larger society, whose culture is viewed as different from that of the majority of the society. Ethnic group members are usually bound together by the common ties of race, nationality or culture, or may believe themselves to be so linked, or are thought to be.

ETHNOCENTRISM

The belief or feeling that one's group has a mode of living, values and patterns of adaptation that are superior to those of other groups. It is often coupled with a generalized contempt for members of other groups.

EUROCENTRISM

A generalized set of beliefs that holds European, especially Western and Central European and English, history, culture and technology as both superior and pivotal to an understanding of the ancient and modern worlds, and an appropriate standard by which to examine and evaluate other societies and cultures that are non-European.

MARGINALITY

Connotes the incomplete assimilation of a group or groups in the larger society.

MASS CULTURE

A consequence of modern economic development which became highly recognizable in the United States during the decade of the 1920s. Connotes the ascendancy of consumption and consumerism as the criterion for self-worth, also the rise of leisure, popular forms of entertainment, advertisement and consumer credit.

MELTING POT

An early-twentieth-century concept with distant antecedents that go back to the beginning of the American Republic. The term gained currency due in part to the 1908 play *The Melting Pot,* by Israel Zangwill. It is associated with the belief that various cultures in a society, particularly the United States, could be fused together.

MONOCULTURALISM

See **Ethnocentrism.**

MULTICULTURALISM

Usually thought of as the existence of different cultures within a society, each with norms, beliefs, behaviors and attitudes that are more or less unique. It has also been used to refer to those areas of human activity that are shared across racial and cultural lines. Some have advanced a more expansive connotation of the term to include the physically challenged, gays, lesbians and bisexuals.

NEW CULTURAL PLURALISM

A contemporary variant on the cultural pluralism first called for in the early twentieth century which recognizes greater particularity among different cultural groups and often advocates various forms of ethnocentrism.

A Selective Survey of Recent Literature on Pluralism in America

Acrimony and confusion over objectives aside, the search for a workable framework for cultural pluralism in the United States has generated some excellent scholarship and polemics in recent years. The most accessible and valuable opuses are the products of academically based scholars. Among the most useful in this study is Arthur Schlesinger, Jr., *The Disuniting of America: Reflections on a Multicultural Society* (New York: W.W. Norton & Company, 1992), which is an eloquent advocacy of traditional pluralism and a stunning critique of the particularist pluralism espoused by ethnocentrists. Although Schlesinger does not closely examine the arts, his analysis of history, ethos and national character are useful to informed arts professionals.

Another important work by one of the more thoughtful pluralists is Henry Louis Gates, Jr., *Loose Canons: Notes on the Culture Wars* (New York: Oxford University Press, 1992), which strikes a balance between ethnocentric radicalism and the protestations of the neoclassicists. Gates is especially insightful and provocative in his examination of the need to expand the American literary canon. Along these lines are an excellent compilation of writings by Americans, with accompanying headnotes on their respective cultural contexts, Gary Colombo, Robert Cullen and Bonnie Lisle, eds., *Rereading America: Cultural Contexts for Critical Thinking and Writing* (New York: Bedford Books, 1989), and Toni Morrison, *Playing in the Dark: Whiteness and the Literary Imagination* (Cambridge: Harvard University Press, 1990). A searing analysis of modern racism in America is found in Chapter 2 of Cornel West, *Prophesy Deliverance! An Afro-American Revolutionary Christianity* (Philadelphia: Westminster Press, 1982), and in Andrew Hacker, *Two Nations: Black and White, Separate, Hostile, Unequal* (New York: Charles Scribner's Sons, 1992).

Deeply personal and often persuasive accounts of ethnic and cultural revelation in the United States may be drawn from Rick Simonson and Scott Walker, eds., *The Graywolf Annual Five: Multi-Cultural Literacy* (Saint Paul: Graywolf Press, 1988). An excellent survey of American culture informed by recent historical scholarship is Stanley Coben and Lorman Ratner, *The Development of an American Culture* (Englewood Cliffs: Prentice-Hall, 1970). An essential text to an understanding of the new cultural pluralism and Afrocentrism is Molefi Kete Asante, *The Afrocentric Idea* (Philadelphia: Temple University Press, 1987). A recently published compilation of essays debating the conflict over American cultural standards is Francis J. Beckwith and

Michael E. Bauman, *Are You Politically Correct?: Debating America's Cultural Standards* (Buffalo: Prometheus Books, 1993). A thoughtful synthetic treatment of the history of cultural debates in modern America is James Davision Hunter, *Culture Wars: The Struggle to Define America* (New York: Basic Books, 1991).

Two exceptionally comprehensive volumes of recent scholarship on the effects of contemporary considerations of culture, patrimony and power on museum collection development, exhibition policies and representation are Ivan Karp and Steven D. Lavine, eds., *Exhibiting Cultures: The Poetics and Politics of Museum Display* (Washington, D.C.: Smithsonian Institution Press, 1991), and Ivan Karp, Christine Mullen Kreamer and Steven D. Lavine, eds., *Museums and Communities: The Politics of Public Culture* (Washington, D.C.: Smithsonian Institution Press, 1992). A compilation of thoughtful and timely essays on the role of pluralism in the visual arts and American culture is Marcia Tucker, ed., *Different Voices: A Social, Cultural, and Historical Framework for Change in the American Art Museum* (New York: Association of Art Museum Directors, 1992). Museum professionals and specialists in Afro-American art would also benefit from ArtTable, Inc., *Race, Ethnicity, and Culture in the Visual Arts* (New York: American Council for the Arts, 1993); National Black Arts Festival, *Selected Essays: Art & Artists from the Harlem Renaissance to the 1980s* (Atlanta: National Black Arts Festival, Inc., 1988); Guy C. McElroy, *Facing History: The Black Image in American Art, 1710-1940* (San Francisco: Bedford Arts, Publishers, 1990); Gary A. Reynolds and Beryl J. Wright, eds., *Against the Odds: African-American Artists and the Harmon Foundation* (Newark: The Newark Museum, 1989), and

Memory and Metaphor: The Art of Romare Bearden, 1940-1987 (New York: Oxford University Press, 1991).

For an understanding of the life and culture of the nation's newest immigrant groups see Albert Camarillo, *Chicanos in a Changing Society* (Cambridge: Harvard University Press, 1979); Elaine Kim, *Introduction to Asian American Literature* (Philadelphia: Temple University Press, 1982); Illsoo Kim, *New Urban Immigrants: The Korean Community in New York* (Princeton: Princeton University Press, 1981); William Peterson, *Japanese Americans: Oppression and Success* (New York: Random House, 1971); David Reimers, *Still the Golden Door: The Third World Comes to New York* (New York: Columbia University Press, 1985); and Eui-Young Yu, et al., eds. *Koreans in Los Angeles* (Los Angeles: California State University Press, 1982).

Recent scholarship on ethnicity among white Americans, particularly the shift away from traditional ethnic blocs and chauvinism by that sector of the population, may be found in Richard D. Alba, *Ethnic Identity: The Transformation of White America* (New Haven: Yale University Press, 1990); Mary C. Waters, *Ethnic Options: Choosing Identities in America* (Berkeley: University of California Press, 1990), and Lawrence H. Fuchs, *The American Kaleidoscope: Race, Ethnicity, and the Civic Culture* (Middletown, Conn.: Wesleyan University Press, 1990). The most ambitious examination of new ethnic sensibilities of racial minorities is Harold Cruse, *Plural but Equal: Blacks and Minorities in America's Plural Society* (New York: William Morrow and Company, Inc., 1987). Still useful in its examination of the mythology surrounding the American melting pot is Philip Gleason, "The Melting Pot: Symbol of Fusion or Confusion?," *American Quarterly* 16 (Spring 1964):20-46.

Neoclassicists have contributed to the culture wars in a number of critiques of cultural pluralism. The neoconservative approach is best articulated in two works, William J. Bennett, *To Reclaim a Legacy: A Report on the Humanities in Higher Education* (Washington, D.C.: National Endowment for the Humanities, 1984), and Allan A. Bloom, *The Closing of the American Mind* (New York: Simon and Schuster, 1987). Among the most useful, even for pluralists, is Roger Kimball, *Tenured Radicals: How Politics Has Corrupted Higher Education* (New York: Harper and Row, 1990), a major study of the ascendancy of radical ethnic politics, Marxism and feminism, and the decline of academic excellence on American college campuses. This controversial line of reasoning is also explored by Hilton Kramer in "The Counter-Revolution Abroad, the Cultural Revolution at Home," *The New Criterion* 10 (September 1991):1-4. Less successful is Dinesh D'Souza, *Illiberal Education: The Politics of Race and Sex on Campus* (New York: The Free Press, 1991).

Among the best critiques of the misuse of the politics of race is Shelby Steele, *The Content of Our Character: A New Vision of Race in America* (New York: St. Martin's Press, 1990), and most recently his article "The New Sovereignty: Grievance Groups Have Become Nations Unto Themselves," *Harper's* (July 1992):47-54. A widely cited argument critical of ethnocentrism is Diane Ravitch, "Multiculturalism: E Pluribus Plures," *The American Scholar* 59 (Summer 1990): 337-354. Professor Ravitch's experiences in the effort to create a multicultural curriculum amid the culture wars is told in Diane Ravitch, "In the Multicultural Trenches," *Contention* 1 (Spring 1992):29-36.

A global perspective on the interrelationship of cultures is found in Thomas Sowell, "A World View of Cultural Diversity,"

Cultural Consensus (November/December 1991):37-44; also by
the same author an earlier analysis of ethnicity, *Ethnic America: A History* (New York: Basic Books, 1981). Another important
work critical of the ethnocentric variant in cultural pluralism
is Henry Louis Gates, Jr., "Beware of the New Pharoahs,"
Newsweek (23 September 1991); on its possible irrelevance to
contemporary problems facing racial minorities see John
Bracey, "Facing Africa: The Price of Our History," *African Com-
mentary* I (November 1989):12-14. The problems associated
with contemporary racial politics in urban America, particularly New York, are brilliantly explored in Jim Sleeper, *The Clos-
est of Strangers: Liberalism and the Politics of Race in New York*
(New York: W.W. Norton & Company, 1990).

The existing literature on the role of cultural pluralism in
contemporary American arts policy and creativity is not nearly
as extensive as writings in education, history and the humanities. The dearth of scholarship in this field may suggest, among
other things, the absence of sharp disagreements over cultural
pluralism among arts interests, the relative immaturity of arts
policy scholarship as a field, or the inaccessibility of extant writings through typical data search efforts. It may also be true
that the profusion of writing on cultural pluralism and multiculturalism in other fields adequately addresses the issues
facing the arts. Nonetheless, there are important works which
are useful to arts interests, including a masterful study of the
development of modern American culture, Lawrence W. Levine,
*Highbrow Lowbrow: The Emergence of Cultural Hierarchy in
America* (Cambridge: Harvard University Press, 1988). Students
of American culture and art would also benefit from Malcolm
Cowley, "The Revolt against Gentility," in *After the Genteel Tradition: American Writers, 1910-1930*, edited by Malcolm Cowley

(1937; repr., Carbondale, Ill.: Illinois University Press, 1964); Herbert I. Schiller, *Culture, Inc.: The Corporate Takeover of Public Expression* (New York: Oxford University Press, 1989); Daniel M. Fox, *Engines of Culture: Philanthropy and Art Museums* (Madison: State Historical Society of Wisconsin, 1963); Raymond Williams, *Culture and Society: 1870-1950* (New York: Harper and Row, 1983); the indispensable Calvin Tomkins, *Merchants and Masterpieces: The Story of the Metropolitan Museum of Art* (New York: E.P. Dutton, 1970); Christopher Lasch, *The Culture of Narcissism: American Life in an Age of Diminishing Expectations* (New York: W.W. Norton and Company, 1978); Edward Kennedy Ellington, *Music Is My Mistress* (Garden City, N.Y.: Doubleday, 1973), and Thomas Bender, "Lionel Trilling and American Culture," *American Quarterly* 42 (June 1990): 324-347, and by the same author, "Negotiating Public Culture: Inclusion and Synthesis," *Liberal Education* 78 (March/April 1992):10-15, and "The Culture of the Metropolis," *Journal of Urban History* 14 (August 1988):492-502. This study has drawn liberally from Lawrence W. Levine, "Jazz and American Culture," *Journal of American Folklore* 102 (January 1989):6-20, which is available in a compilation of the author's recent essays, *The Unpredictable Past: Explorations in American Cultural History* (New York: Oxford University Press, 1993).

Although lacking an analytical framework, valuable insights into arts policy shaped by cultural pluralist ideals and practices are found in The National Task Force on Presenting and Touring the Performing Arts, *An American Dialogue* (Washington, D.C.: Association of Performing Arts Presenters, 1989). A survey of initiatives promoting cultural pluralism in the arts is National Assembly of State Arts Agencies, *Report of the NASAA Task Force on Cultural Pluralism* (Washington, D.C.: National

Assembly of State Arts Agencies, 1989); also, for a reliable compilation of multicultural arts groups, see Johanna L. Misey, ed., *National Directory of Multi-Cultural Arts Organizations* (Washington, D.C.: National Assembly of State Arts Agencies, 1990). Results of a 1990 survey of multicultural arts centers are published in Elinor Bowles, *Cultural Centers of Color* (Washington, D.C.: National Endowment for the Arts, 1992). One of the best of recent scholarly studies in the field is Jean J. Schensul, "Organizing Cultural Diversity Through the Arts," *Education and Urban Society* 22 (August 1990):377-392. For the most ambitious examination of arts education in contemporary American life see National Endowment for the Arts, *Toward Civilization: A Report on Arts Education* (Washington, D.C.: U.S. Government Printing Office, 1988). A succinct yet wonderfully conceptualized vision of a diversified arts environment in California is found in The 2000 Partnership, *Our Many Voices: A New Composition* (Los Angeles: The 2000 Partnership, 1991).

Sources

Chapter One

Ronald Takaki, ed., *From Different Shores: Perspectives on Race and Ethnicity in America* (New York: Oxford University Press, 1987).

Gary B. Nash, *Red, White, and Black: The People of Early America* (Englewood Cliffs: Prentice-Hall, 1974), Chapters 4, 7.

Joan W. Scott, "Liberal Historians: A Unitary Vision," *The Chronicle of Higher Education* XXXVII (September 11, 1991): B1-2.

Simon Schama, "Clio Has a Problem," *The New York Times Magazine,* 8 September 1991:30-34.

Arthur M. Schlesinger, Jr., *The Disuniting of America: Reflections on a Multicultural Society* (New York: W.W. Norton and Company, 1992), pp. 23-72.

Winthrop D. Jordan, *White Over Black: American Attitudes Toward the Negro, 1550-1812* (Baltimore: Penguin, 1969), p. 542.

W.E.B. DuBois, *The Souls of Black Folk* (New York: Dutton, 1969), p. xxxi.

Nathan Glazer and Daniel Patrick Moynihan, *Beyond the Melting Pot: The Negroes, Puerto Ricans, Jews, Italians, and Irish of New York City* (Cambridge: Massachusetts Institute of Technology Press, 1963).

Shelby Steele, *The Content of Our Character: A New Vision of Race in America* (New York: St. Martin's Press, 1990).

Chapter Two

Andrew Hacker, "Trans-National America," *The New York Review of Books*, 22 November 1990:19-24.

Rayford W. Logan, *The Betrayal of the Negro: From Rutherford B. Hayes to Woodrow Wilson* (New York: Collier, 1967).

Nathan Irwin Huggins, *Harlem Renaissance* (New York: Oxford University Press, 1971), Chapter 2.

Daniel Joseph Singal, "Towards a Definition of American Modernism," in *Modernist Culture in America,* ed. Daniel Joseph Singal (Belmont, Calif.: Wadsworth Publishing Co., 1991), pp. 1-23.

Houston A. Baker, Jr., "Modernism and the Harlem Renaissance," in *Modernist Culture in America,* pp. 107-124.

Edward P. Alexander, *Museum Masters: Their Museums and Their Influence* (Nashville: American Association for State and Local History, 1978), pp. 379-406.

Steven D. Lavine, "Museums and Multiculturalism: Who Is In Control?" *Museum News* (March/April 1989):36-44.

John Von Rhein, "A Chicago Century," *Symphony Magazine* 42 (1 May 1991):23-26.

Lawrence W. Levine, "Jazz and American Culture," *Journal of American Folklore* 102 (January 1989):6-20.

Lawrence W. Levine, *Highbrow/Lowbrow: The Emergence of Cultural Hierarchy in America* (Cambridge: Harvard University Press, 1988), Chapters 2-3.

Gary A. Reynolds, "American Critics and the Harmon Foundation Exhibitions," in *Against the Odds: African-American Artists and the Harmon Foundation*, eds. Gary A. Reynolds and Beryl J. Wright (Newark: The Newark Museum, 1989), pp. 107-118.

Chapter Three

Andrew Hacker, "Trans-National America," *The New York Review of Books*, 22 November 1990:19.

Molefi Kete Asante, "Multiculturalism: An Exchange," *The American Scholar* 60 (Spring 1991):269-272.

Molefi Kete Asante, *The Afrocentric Idea* (Philadelphia: Temple University Press, 1987), pp. 3-18.

Thomas Sowell, "A World View of Cultural Diversity," *Cultural Consensus* 29 (1 November 1991):37-42.

Arthur M. Schlesinger, Jr., *The Disuniting of America: Reflections on a Multicultural Society,* pp. 43, 102.

Diane Ravitch, "Multiculturalism, E Pluribus Plures," *American Scholar* 59 (Summer 1990):337-354.

Diane Ravitch, "Multiculturalism: An Exchange," *American Scholar* 60 (Spring 1991):272-276.

Diane Ravitch, "In the Multicultural Trenches," *Contention* 1 (Spring 1992):29-36.

Gary B. Nash, "The Great Multicultural Debate," *Contention* 1 (Spring 1992):1-28.

Frederic Smoler, "What Should We Teach Our Children About American History?" an interview with Arthur M. Schlesinger, Jr., *American Heritage* (February/March 1992):45-52.

Adam Begley, "Henry Louis Gates, Jr., Black Studies' New Star," *The New York Times Magazine,* 1 April 1990:24-27, 48-50.

Richard D. Alba, *Ethnic Identity: The Transformation of White America* (New Haven: Yale University Press, 1990).

Mary C. Waters, *Ethnic Options: Choosing Identities in America* (Berkeley: University of California Press, 1990).

Roger Kimball, "Tenured Radicals: A Postscript," *The New Criterion* 10 (January 1991):4-15.

Jesse M. Vazquez, "On the Language and Ideology of the New Multiculturalism: Rhetoric and Substance," keynote address given to the symposium on Museums and Multicultural Change, 5 October 1990, Princeton, N.J.

Hilton Kramer, "The Counter-Revolution Abroad, the Cultural Revolution at Home," *The New Criterion* 10 (September 1991):1-4.

Catherine R. Stimpson, "Big Man on Campus," a review of Dinesh D'Souza, *Illiberal Education: The Politics of Race and Sex on Campus, The Nation*, 30 September 1991:378-384.

Howard Risatti, "Culturally Correct Criteria?" *New Art Examiner* (October 1991):25-28.

Roger Kimball, "Vistas of Inanity: Art and Ideas in the Eighties," *The New Criterion* 9 (April 1990):38-43.

A. E. Barnes, "Blaspheming Like Brutal Beasts: Multiculturalism From An Historical Perspective," *Contention* 1 (Spring 1992):37-58.

Thomas Bender, "Negotiating Public Culture: Inclusion and Synthesis in American History," *Liberal Education* 78 (March/April 1992):10-15

Chapter Four

Willard L. Boyd, "Cultural Understanding and Respect Through the Arts," speech given at the Annual Meeting of the Illinois Arts Alliance, 6 June 1991.

John J. O'Connor, "For the Right, TV Is Half the Battle," Arts & Leisure Section, *The New York Times*, 14 June 1992, pp. 1, 24.

American Council for the Arts, *Developing Multicultural Boards: Experiences and Opportunities*, meeting at the Japanese American Cultural and Community Center, Los Angeles, California (New York: American Council for the Arts, 1990), pp. 1-8.

A. B. Spellman, "The New Pluralism," *The Challenge of Change: Papers and Presentations from the 15th Annual National Conference of FEDAPT* (New York: FEDAPT, 1987), pp. 83-86.

Michalann Hobson, "A Marketing Manifesto," *The Challenge of Change,* pp. 101-110.

The National Task Force on Presenting and Touring the Performing Arts, *An American Dialogue* (Washington, D.C.: Association of Performing Arts Presenters, 1989), pp. 13-17, 57-64.

The 2000 Partnership, *Our Many Voices: A New Composition* (Los Angeles: The 2000 Partnership, 1991).

Jean J. Schensul, "Organizing Cultural Diversity Through the Arts," *Education and Urban Society* 22 (August 1990):377-392.

Robert Garfias, "Cultural Diversity and the Arts in America," in *Public Money and the Muse: Essays on Government Funding for the Arts,* ed. Stephen Benedict (New York: W.W. Norton and Company, 1991), pp. 182-194.

Arturo Madrid, "Diversity and Its Discontents," *Academe, Bulletin of the American Association of University Professors* (November/December 1990):15-19.

Chapter Five

Queens Museum of Art, *Newsletter,* Summer 1992:1.

Mechal Sobel, *The World They Made Together: Black and White Values in Eighteenth-Century Virginia* (Princeton: Princeton University Press, 1987), p. 5.

National Assembly of State Arts Agencies, *Report of the NASAA Task Force on Cultural Pluralism* (Washington, D.C.: National Assembly of State Arts Agencies, 1989).

Thomas Bender, "Negotiating Public Culture: Inclusion and Synthesis in American History," p. 15.

About the American Council for the Arts

Founded in 1960, the American Council for the Arts (ACA) is a national organization whose purpose is to define issues and promote public policies that advance the contributions of the arts and the artist to American life. To accomplish its mission, ACA conducts research, sponsors conferences and public forums, publishes books, reports, and periodicals, advocates before Congress for legislation that benefits the arts, and maintains a 15,000-volume specialized library. ACA is one of the nation's primary sources of legislative news affecting all of the arts and serves as a leading advisor to arts administrators, individual artists, educators, elected officials, arts patrons and the general public.